PRIDE AND PURPOSE

PRIDE AND PURPOSE

The Genesis of Competent Leadership

Priya Somaiya

BLOOMSBURY
NEW DELHI • LONDON • OXFORD • NEW YORK • SYDNEY

BLOOMSBURY INDIA
Bloomsbury Publishing India Pvt. Ltd
Second Floor, LSC Building No. 4, DDA Complex, Pocket C – 6 & 7,
Vasant Kunj, New Delhi 110070

BLOOMSBURY, BLOOMSBURY INDIA and the Diana logo
are trademarks of Bloomsbury Publishing Plc

This edition published in 2020

ISBN: HB: 978-93-90077-89-2; eBook: 978-93-90077-91-5

2 4 6 8 10 9 7 5 3 1

Typeset in Manipal Technologies Limited
Printed and bound in India by Sanat Printers, Kundli, Haryana

CONTENTS

Introduction

In my professional experience of almost four decades, I came to know of leaders with exceptional talent who led people and organisations effectively. They stood out as highly capable people with extraordinary qualities. These qualities took them into leadership roles in the organisations where they worked and contributed immensely. This book is a compilation of my observations on leaders and leadership.

Pride and Purpose is not based on any systematic research and, therefore, I cannot claim any conclusive and scientific deductions on leadership. The chapters enclosed in this book contain descriptions of human qualities which, in my understanding, also contribute in shaping leadership behaviours.

This book has been written keeping in mind the long view, which means that some qualities that I describe assist the leadership process to unfold gradually. Leading is a process comprised of communication, decision-making, motivating, inspiring, monitoring and reviewing. The focus on goals, results and all the various activities of execution and implementation also form an integral part of leading. Effective leaders involve the team in all work processes and largely concentrate on facilitation and themselves, thereby creating feelings of commitment and ownership in team members. The leadership process also has a deep and lasting impact on people, events and other processes at workplace and in society at large. People who lead wonderfully well inevitably orchestrate long-term impact and a great depth of change in those around them. And on many occasions, the qualities of leaders are the real game-changers for organisational, social and personal transformation.

Leaders shape the behaviour and the thinking of those with whom they work through coaching, mentoring, inspiring and influencing. We have extensive literature on coaching and mentoring in various parts of the world, and many leaders aspire to become good coaches and mentors too. A large number of leaders acquire coaching and mentoring skills which go a long way in shaping the potential and talent of the younger generation. These skills also help in developing high-performing teams in organisations. I will be continually referring to these skills in a number of chapters and also will be considering them interchangeable with leadership. I had the privilege to observe these skills in the workplace and, therefore, will be sharing my own experiences of leaders who coached and mentored me.

I have deliberately stayed away from the debate around the role of heredity and environment. However, socialisation and learning do play a major role in the genesis of leadership qualities and behaviours. Emulation, observation, experiencing and interacting, I also believe, are significant learning processes for the development of leadership skills. Leadership qualities can develop at any age in a person's life. It is my belief that a human being is a dynamic entity. The cells of the human body are continuously changing, and without us even being aware of it, we do acquire a new body over the course of several years. What a great marvel of nature. If this change and transformation can happen at the physiological level, then why not at the psychological, self or behavioural level as well?! Therefore, it is highly likely that personality changes, emergence of certain qualities and behaviours, and the disappearance of some can happen at any age. So is it with leadership qualities and behaviours. It is also true that we need time and space to work with our qualities, competencies and skills. Leadership qualities also tend to erode if they do not find the right place and opportunity to be applied and utilised. Even though leadership behaviours can be learnt at any age, if people are given learning opportunities and responsibilities when they are younger, it is likely that these qualities and behaviours begin to take shape, and strong, sustainable and long-lasting behaviours develop earlier on in life. These behaviours, when utilised and demonstrated, facilitate the person in achieving great success in leading. The person can mentor and coach others to imbibe these qualities and can influence more and more people in their family, workplace and in the communities around them. At the operational level, these qualities also assist the person to take the team along. Great leaders have developed in this way, and in business and national history, we have a number of such examples. To name a few are Martin Luther King, Mahatma Gandhi, Jamshedji Tata and the great emperor, Akbar.

Unknown poor widows in the villages of India are also leaders in their own right. They take the responsibility to earn for their fatherless young children, inspire them to work hard and study well, thereby leading them to a better and secure future. Leadership, therefore, is not all about name, fame, popularity or great wealth. People who are famous may not be good leaders and vice versa. Leaders, however, do achieve outstandingly well in work and also in their social lives. Leadership is not about position or authority. One can lead from any formal or informal position in an organisation, family or society. It is largely about impact and influence and steering teams, whether in the organisation or in the family, towards a better future. Leaders work for the future, whether it is the political, technological, social, cultural or spiritual future. It is also true that all these dimensions of the future intersect at various points.

Leadership is a process which facilitates the journey to a destination. People who play a major role in that journey are the leaders. At no point or time can we underestimate the contribution of the followers in their success and achievement. This is not an individual journey. It is a journey which many people choose to undertake together. Leaders assist in the choice of a destination for the people they lead and journey towards the destination with their teams. They walk with the others and often walk in front to show the way. They clear the weeds, remove the roadblocks and also weather the storms that arise on the path.

In this book, I have approached leadership through the lens of leadership qualities. This is by no means an attempt to go back to the trait model of leadership and espouse the trait model as the only sensible approach to understanding leadership. There are many thoughts on the matter, many processes examined and innumerable models and frameworks developed and discussed around the world in corporations, organisations and in academia. The leadership style model and the situational model of leadership are interesting and useful models too. All the models are thought-provoking. Our approaches and beliefs on leadership, therefore, will keep reflecting the evolution of thought in the areas which, in turn, are influenced by the complexity and the developments of the events that happen with us and around us in this world.

There was a time when leadership behaviour and qualities were put in the framework of power and authority, and it was thought that leadership was all about these qualities. It also depended upon where the followers were in their thinking, beliefs, emotions and behaviour. Today, the followers respond to authority in a different way and, perhaps, positional power is no longer the sole source for leadership legitimacy. It is the collegial leadership model and the stewardship of the organisation that leaders and followers are discovering more effective approaches or paradigms. The leadership behaviours in the partnership model are found more fitting by followers now than the positional power model. Leaders are preferred as mentors and coaches rather than as only authority figures.

In fact, I believe that leadership skills and competencies are equally important when compared with qualities and traits of the person concerned. Qualities could also become the basis of specific and sharpened skills and competencies. For example, courage as a quality could become the anchor of taking judicious decisions and taking risks with financial investments. In some chapters of this book, you will find that leadership qualities are also connected and integrated with skills and processes. For example, the feeling of pride and the clarity, understanding and acceptance of purpose have facilitated many leaders and organisations to craft a compelling vision for the organisation. A well-crafted vision inspires pride and once the vision and the purpose are communicated to the entire organisation, leaders in many positions in the organisation will be able to mobilise remarkable achievements and results. Qualities and traits are, at times, demonstrated as attitudes also. Another example could be personal motivation. High energy sustains motivation through effort, hard work and persistence.

Leaders also require a lot of energy to motivate and inspire others, and this energy keeps their own motivation, resilience and persistence levels high. To arouse passion and inspiration in others about their work and goals, leaders must themselves be passionate and inspired. The skills to motivate, communicate in a way to arouse passion, commitment and inspiration cannot happen without energy. Once passion and inspiration is high, it leads to more energised involvement with work. Therefore, all the facets of leadership, be it personal qualities or skills and competencies or styles and processes, must synergise with each other. I chose the trait and quality route because, primarily, it is simple and it helped me to fit my direct experiences into this framework.

Very little thought appears to have been applied to the area of followership. Without followers, the concept of leadership cannot be understood or even utilised. In fact, the concepts of leadership and followership are interdependent. Both the concepts have to be understood in a relational paradigm. The two roles completely complement each other and cannot be conceptualised separately. Followership is indeed an extremely significant role and manifests in various behaviours which facilitate the expression or the enactment of the leadership role itself. There are immense advantages if both the roles are facilitative of each other.

The roles of the leaders as well as the followers and the leader–follower partnerships evolve over time and are dynamic. The elements in the concepts have changed and the dimensions in the relationship and the partnership have also changed and are ever-evolving. Today, leadership is not viewed narrowly through a single myopic lens of positional authority, instructional commands, seniority in age or hierarchy or the power to dole out monetary or other material rewards. Similarly, followership has acquired a wider meaning and is not defined only in terms of execution of the commands of the leader without questioning them and accepting all the guidance given by the leader in silence and acquiescence. Without the questions and debates of a modern, contemporary or an evolved partnership that is accepted by both, the leader–follower partnership will not work today.

Followers are responsible for bringing out the best in leaders. It is through and with them that leaders manage processes, craft and design plans, construct and select strategies, and implement and execute work plans. Followers share the leadership platform and the mandate equally. They bring their own valued expertise and professional experience, and are leaders in their areas in their own right. In day-to-day work, there are also role reversals when leaders follow the followers during a project, a meeting or a discussion. Followers assume the leadership role, show the direction, influence and instruct, and manage complex processes because of their expertise, competence and skills in certain valued and required areas of performance.

The leadership process is, therefore, ever evolving and is a fascinating interplay of human qualities, skills, knowledge, wisdom and attitudes. The process unfolds in the larger social, cultural and organisational context in which leaders and followers endeavour to impact and drive change and development. The relationship between leaders and followers is crucial in embedding processes and actions for achieving goals and results. Both leaders and followers discover that not only are the future goals inspiring but the journey towards the goals is equally so.

Pride and Purpose

I wonder what it will be like if there is a continuous feeling of pride in us that one is alive and that life has a purpose. A number of us aspire for it but don't seem to have it or even if we have it for a while it vanishes with great speed the next minute. The fundamental work of great leaders is in the area of pride and purpose. They contribute largely in discovering the purpose behind life, work, institutions, organisations and human endeavour. They also help us in engaging with the purpose and attaining the tasks that emanate from it in such a way that makes us feel proud of ourselves, our work, our efforts and what we achieve.

Pride is anchored in feelings of high self-esteem and a valued reputation. Pride is a positive feeling which results from attaining the purpose and doing things and putting in the effort that is guided by purpose. Purpose is inherent in our efforts of striving for that which is good and directing our efforts towards it. Living with pride, therefore, would mean that the person is engaged with work and tasks which lead to aspired results and value. The opportunity to be engaged in significant work and contribute beyond expectations appear to be goals worth pursuing.

Life is not a straight line or a journey on a smooth and straight road. If that were the case then it wouldn't be difficult to see well into the future. More memories of the past would remain with us for a longer time as the road behind would be more visible when we journeyed ahead. Life, as we know, is a road full of twists and turns. Therefore, most of the time we don't know for certain what lies ahead or around the turn. What is left behind also becomes invisible as the new twists and turns block the rear view. This establishes the unpredictability of life and puts more strain on us all, but also demands greater and more conscious effort to carry forward the great legacies and inheritance of the past. The unpredictability and uncertainty of life is one of the many prime motivators for us.

When we do an analysis of all the motivators behind living and our efforts we can well say that it is the challenge of the unknown, the uncertainty of what lies ahead or what destiny will bring for us is the prime force compelling us to keep preparing for the future. Our lives are dominated by our thinking, visualisation, excitement, passion and, more importantly, by fear and anxiety. Fear and anxiety are powerful emotions. Most of the time we grapple with emotions which are related to distant events that are yet to happen and over which we don't have full control. If we're always trying to actualise our future and not living in the present, we don't get to experience a feeling of pride. Those who live in the future most of the time don't have the free mental space for living with fearlessness and pride. Often, our entire mental space is occupied with the negative emotions like fear, panic and anxiety. These emotions are powerful and pervasive that grip the mind and the heart and force us to think negatively.

Pride is all about the present. Pride is actually celebrating the present and having a wholesome contentment with the goodness of the present. It is the power of the now and all the perceived advantages available in that now that pride is meant to celebrate. It is important to understand the difference between contentment and complacency. When there is a feeling of appreciation and gratitude for all that is available with us from which we can beget wholesomeness and joy in the present, we experience contentment. Being complacent is not being attentive, not bothering about the good and the bad, drifting without focus, and having low energy and motivation and little joy. It means living with a sense of resignation which creates frustration and cynicism.

To be contented is to validate the present with pride and also validate ourselves in our present, positive reality. Pride blossoms in the validated present with all its achievements, advantages, gifts and affirmations. It is the spirit of living out the present and knowing the strengths of the present. When we see a proud nation, the proud citizens of a country, parents and children and mentors and coaches, we know that all of them have recognised the gifts and the spirit of the present.

We cannot be proud about the future because we don't know it; the future has not happened and we await it. We can be proud of the past and its goodness because the gifts can be, and often are, carried into the present in our memory and in the cultural archetype.

However, the past lives in our memory. The present lives now with us and is palpable in the moment. We always and actually breathe in the moment. People who don't live in the present don't actually know the essence of pride and don't smell its pervading fragrance. Most times, we prefer to escape it and live in the past or the future. We are anxiously preoccupied with the future and live with fear or anxiety or with the resentment and guilt of the past. We keep destroying the present and, therefore, keep throttling pride and its infectious positivity. A number of people in their entire life don't experience it at all. In other words, they don't experience the present because life can only be contained in pride to be lived in the present as every moment has so much to celebrate. Breathing itself is celebration to be grateful for and to be positively astonished about. We are connected with the universe only through the pride in the moment. Pride can be experienced when we are truly and fully alive.

Preserving Pride

I was sitting with a friend and her family one summer evening. The family of my friend were well-to-do business people, well-educated and cultured. Apart from being involved with the business, the entire family was also immersed in varied interests and hobbies. There was a genuine appreciation of music, art, craft and reading. Most members of the family were very well-read and well-informed. It was a pleasure spending the evening with them because the conversations were so thought-provoking and educative. However, there was one male family member in his mid-forties who was quite different from the rest. He was the whiz-kid in business, very ambitious and also tended to be abrasive in his interactions and overall communication. He had contributed the most to the success of the family business and was, therefore, admired—almost held in awe—and feared.

My friend and I were having a friendly chat and enjoying our lemonade when the children returned from their tuition classes. It was also the day when their examination results were declared. The daughter had fared better than the son, and his father had already admonished him on the phone from his office.

He was the son of the same abrasive family member, and my friend was his wife. My friend looked at her son with a lot of affection and a little concern when he came in. She asked him about his results and wanted to see the marksheet. As he took out the sheet, the father walked in; seeing him, the boy almost froze to the ground. The father took long strides towards us and immediately snatched the marksheet from his wife and sat on the chair, opposite the son, stiffly and with a lot of authority. As he browsed through the marks, his facial expression turned more aggressive and angry and then in a booming voice, full of disgust and disdain, he declared that the son had fared very badly in his mathematics examination and that a mere 73 per cent was not acceptable. According to him, mathematics is a scoring subject, and an intelligent person scores full marks. My friend gently reminded him that he should also see and understand that the son had scored 98 per cent in social studies, 94 per cent in English language and literature, and in all other papers, he scored between 89 and 94 per cent. He said he was not concerned with it and that the way the son was performing in mathematics, he would not be able to clear entrance examinations for any of the reputed engineering and medical colleges. He was extremely worried about his final result and how he would manage future admission opportunities. Pronouncing his verdict, he rose from the chair and went away, informing his wife that he would be travelling the day after for work and that she must take the responsibility of preparing the children to do much better in the future. Life, he said, was not easy and the future was going to become more and more competitive.

In a moment, and with one stroke of abrasiveness and insensitivity, the father managed to tear the present into smithereens only to construct a dismal future full of anxiety and failure and smudging it with shame and guilt. All the beauty and richness of the present which was shining through so many numbers and percentages on the report card showing hope and confidence were demolished in a second. The numbers in English and other subjects reflected the strengths and the gifts of the son to be proud of and to cherish and celebrate. The son, his mother and, in fact, the entire family was pushed into an anxious future and a guilt-ridden past.

This is how inferiority is created by ignoring some aspects of reality. Pride is anchored in the present reality—factual, concrete and a tangible reality based on facts and figures. The beauty of this reality is that it is largely inside ourselves and contains both strengths and weaknesses and our successes and failures. The present is made up of all this. However, our tendency is to perceive the negatives more. We tend to focus on the weaknesses, failures and threats and not the positives which are the strengths, successes and opportunities. We perceive the negatives because of fear, and fear turns into anxiety, and anxiety takes us to the uncertainties and the imagined catastrophes of the future. The more we think about the negatives, the more prone we become to think in that manner. When we think negatively, we move away from the feelings of pride and joy. The mental space which rightfully belongs to positivity and pride is usurped by anxiety, fear, shame and guilt.

We, as human beings, are meant to manage contradiction and complexity. This makes us grow and spiritually evolve. When we are able to face and manage contradiction and complexity, we feel proud of ourselves. Let me explain this in more detail. Reality is never simple. Life is not simple. We have to manage the feeling of being alive in the moment and the thought that we will die one day in that moment too. We know that we have done well in some areas and in others we have not fared well. We know that some people like us and some don't. These are the contradictions that we must live with and also manage.

In every moment, there lies both an opportunity and a challenge at the same time. We have to understand and prepare ourselves to manage both. Pride enhances the feeling of wellbeing and provides the courage to face reality. Our reality is like a beautiful mosaic with patterns of negatives and positives, and we feel proud acknowledging this reality with calm and wisdom. Leaders facilitate this level of understanding and help in the handling of life and work.

My friend's husband saw only the negative dimensions. He tried to convey the same understanding to his son. He negated the positives that were available in abundance in the moment when he read the report card. He didn't actually read the report card—he couldn't understand and comprehend the entire result and the enormity of success and the opportunities written all over it. His narrow focus on the 73 per cent in mathematics was so emotionally overpowering that in his anxiety and insecurity, he failed to understand the reality and appreciate what was in front of him and his son in that moment. Even factual data was completely ignored. He moved away from reality to a position of inferiority. He told his son that he has not done well at all and if he continued to perform like this then he won't be able to qualify for admissions in engineering or medical colleges.

The father didn't even know what the aspirations of the son were and what other immense opportunities were possible for his son's career. Moreover, the only way for the son to improve his performance in mathematics was through knowledge and awareness about what helped him do so well in other subjects and transfer that learning and core competence in the preparation for mathematics. The best way forward was to utilise the boy's present available strengths, his feeling of pride and confidence, in order to improve in the area which needed attention. We can only overcome weaknesses through our present available strengths. Weaknesses can never be overcome with weaknesses and feelings of diffidence, guilt, shame and anxiety. Positivity and pride motivate us to surmount difficulties and face challenges. Leaders who achieve and face great challenges help maintaining the high level of self-confidence of the team. They facilitate the team to have a grounded, complete and comprehensive understanding of reality. Pride generates modesty and balance. Modesty is the other side of pride because both are inspired by what is real. Strengths are real as much as weaknesses are. The mosaic will always be there. We can't wish it away. That is the nature of life.

Arrogance is immodesty and is not to be confused with pride. The latter is contained in modesty which is in the grain and fabric of pride. If the father had said that the son's report card was perfect and that his mathematics result was on account of the teacher's negative bias in the distribution of marks and that his son is, in fact, a genius like him in mathematics then this would have been showing arrogance. This would also have shown a negation of reality, not appreciating it and taking necessary action. With this stand, the father could also convey to the son that he would get better marks next time without even putting in more effort and the problem to be tackled would have been to win the favour of the teacher instead. Perhaps, in the next breath, the father could have also said that his money, power and connections would get the son better marks and an admission in any college later. This would have been a complete disconnect from reality and extreme arrogance which would have the potential for creating feelings of untested and unwarranted superiority, immodesty, over-confidence and delusions of power and influence. On careful examination, we will realise that inferiority and superiority both come from the negation of reality. Both have their roots in fear and insecurity and both are convenient routes to escape from taking responsibility. Responsibility is an offshoot of pride and confidence.

Pride is a very natural and a normal mental and emotional state. There are, however, varying levels and degrees of pride. When we reach high levels of quality, innovativeness, creativity and path-breaking performances, our pride increases on the basis of what we have achieved. However, even a little improvement instils pride and gives us the confidence to move ahead. Therefore, we must measure pride on a continuum of low to high. It is also necessary to sustain pride and not let the level dip. When we sustain our performance levels and our related confidence and feelings of efficacy, pride is sustained. Positive affirmations, clarity of understanding, facilitation by coaches, mentors and parents, and a constructive and realistic assessment of failures and successes sustain pride.

There is very little pride in today's world and very low engagement with purpose. People talk a lot about satisfaction, happiness, motivation, energy and engagement. On the other hand, ambitions, success, achievements and aspirations are spoken of more than purpose. Therefore, consciously people don't engage with pride or purpose. They appear to be esoteric mental and emotional states for most people.

Somewhere far into later life, people seem to be saying I will engage with pride or purpose now. Youth, and even middle age, is meant to chase worldly success and ambitions and pursue careers which will provide opportunities to earn big money, name and fame. Pride and purpose is for the old; those who are about to retire and who are ready for a life of spirituality or social service. Hence, most years are lived and spent with very little pride or purpose.

Positive pride is different from vanity. Vanity arises from exaggerated self-importance and feelings of superiority. Pride has a component of healthy self-esteem which produces feelings of self-confidence, faith in one's ability to meet challenges, and surmount difficulty and achieve stretched goals and targets. Pride in the team or in the nation simply means holding the team and nation in high esteem, believing in their capability to engage with purpose, meaningful work and goals and in the fact that they can attain these goals.

Pride also reflects values and principles. If courage is valued, then a life lived with courage will give a person a sense of pride. If honesty is valued then a life which is lived with honesty and integrity will create feelings of high self-esteem and pride in the person and such a life will also be perceived to be providing meaning and purpose. Pride is the mental state which results from the congruence of values, principles and actions. If people value honesty and they work and live with honesty, then there is congruence between what they value and what they do. This creates alignment and congruence, and the outcome is self-pride and self-esteem.

Pride which is anchored in a larger purpose is more lasting than motivation and success from wealth, position and power. In pride and purpose, the intrinsic qualities of a person, the values and the connected large goals are admired and the meaning or the purpose, most of the time, is the goal itself. Meaning is an end in itself and not the things that are derived from it. It is the responsibility of leaders to create self-pride, pride in the team, organisation and nation, and in the final analysis, in the entire world order. It is also their work to facilitate the discovery of meanings that are sought out of life and work. Motivation from the source of pride and purpose is permanent and it is the only way to sustain inspiration, commitment and creative contribution.

I

Unmitigated Respect

I was travelling in a village in the forests of the Nilgiri Hills which are in the southern state of Karnataka in South India. These hills are called the Nilgiris because if seen from a distance, they appear to be blue. *Nil* in Hindi or Sanskrit denotes the colour blue. They are thick, dense forests with a variety of fauna and flora. There are a number of ancient Indian tribes residing in the forest. This story is about one such tribe which is known all over India, if not all over the world, for their quaint culture and lifestyle and their wonderful craft which is exquisite hand embroidery. They embroider in just three colours—black, red and white—and use cross stitch only. Their patterns, designs and motifs are their own. It is the creation of their own visualisation and thinking about beauty and elegance, and are not usually copied and used by others. Today, their embroidered shawls, scarfs and dress material are available all over South India in well-known stores selling ethnic products and handicrafts.

This tribal community worships the forest. They don't fell trees or destroy the forest. They only collect old, dry leaves or anything that appears to be discarded. Before commencing any work, they seek permission from the forest through quaint rituals and revere the forest most sincerely.

I was fortunate to have interacted with this tribe of wonderful human beings. One breezy and pleasant afternoon, I had the opportunity to drive into the forest with a few colleagues. We had a driver who belonged to that area and knew the tribe and its ways intimately. As we went into the dense part of the forest we saw a girl in her teens in a navy blue and white school uniform, with hair neatly plaited, walking all alone with great confidence on the road which would have scared the likes of us if we were left alone on that road. Our driver stopped the car and in the tribal language, which he spoke fluently, asked her to jump into the vehicle beside him. The girl thanked him and took the lift in the car happily. We had to drive for another good four to five kilometres. I asked the driver whether the girl walked that far every day. He said yes and informed us that she was a good student and was studying in the ninth standard. She also had plans for higher studies. We came to know that it took the girl almost two hours of walking back from the school to her home daily and when she was late in school she reached home after seven in pitch darkness. We would have died out of fear if we had to walk through the forest in the dark.

As we moved on in our vehicle, I was enthralled to see the beauty of the forest. The fragrance of the trees, the wild flowers and berries was intoxicating. The driver and the girl were talking in the language spoken by the tribe. All of a sudden, the car halted and the girl got down from the car. The driver told us that the girl will come back into the vehicle after she has walked around the large boulder right in the middle of the road. The boulder was smooth on the surface and was about 12–14 inches high and our car slid over the stone easily and crossed it without any trouble. I asked the driver the reason for the girl wanting to walk around the boulder. He said that since they worship the forest they cannot disrespect anything that is a part of the forest and hence she couldn't keep sitting in the car while the vehicle drove over it. This would mean virtually disrespecting the forest God. The tribe values the forest and whatever happens, it is their responsibility to protect and preserve it. At least this is what they think and this is how they live and work. They don't break a single branch, don't pluck flowers or leaves. They only collect fallen fruit or leaves and consider this as the *prasadam* from the forest. All the streams, rivers and tributaries are preserved and protected and not contaminated. Not a single animal or bird is killed. The tribal community is vegetarian and they exist on the agricultural produce that they obtain from farming.

We drove to the tribal settlement. The architecture of the houses was fascinating; something that I had never seen before. They were made out of mud with very low entrances. Leaves, mud and twigs were used for the construction of the doors and the entire house was embellished with beautifully painted motifs depicting the trees, animals, birds and flowers of the forest.

As our car drove into the middle of the tribal hamlet, we saw a number of groups of women sitting together and embroidering on shawls and scarfs. I walked across and sat under a huge banyan tree amongst one of the groups. The driver played the role of an interpreter. I was told that they do embroidery of intricate motifs and designs on large shawls as teams and the elderly who have years of the experience in the craft are the mentors and coaches. The elderly women looked like they were in their late seventies and eighties and walked tall. They looked stately and enjoyed a powerful status in the tribe because the tribe had a matriarchal culture.

When I asked them whether the embroidery could be in other colours, they said that I must understand that the colours represented their identity, their ancestors and their roots. Under no circumstance will the colours change. The driver informed us that the tribe has a history of non-violence, no theft and crime, and they believe in telling the truth. They are a very proud people and respect their women who play an active social leadership role and have a voice in all important decisions concerning individuals, families and the entire tribal community. However, the introduction of television, smartphones and social media is playing havoc amongst the young boys and girls of the tribe. The elders are worried about their tastes, inclinations and behavioural changes.

The story was that two days prior to our arrival, a young boy had broken a branch of a nearby tree and was trying to make a set of wickets with his group of friends when he decided to play cricket that afternoon. On coming to know this, the elders of the community sat together and began to wail and ask forgiveness from the tree and the forest. They were really worried about the changing times and the early signs of doom and destruction. Pride and purpose, they said, was shifting gear, and they were very unhappy about it.

Pride and purpose are the greatest catalysts and agents of change and transformation. Organisational transformations and even individual-level change do not happen if not inspired by a sense of pride in the values and the goals of that aspired change. Large-scale transformation is anchored in a large encompassing purpose of which the role models are the leaders who walk that path with their followers, colleagues and the other torchbearers.

2

Lessons from the Family

The greatest lessons of life come from leaders who make you realise the significance of the strength gained from a life lived with self-pride and anchored in larger meanings and purpose. I was fortunate to find both from the leaders in my family.

Transformation of individuals and organisations is not always planned. It is largely inspired and is also guided by pride and purpose. A number of Hindu Brahmin families fled from Kashmir during periods of forceful mass religious conversions. These families left everything that they owned in Kashmir and went away to save their religious identity. They were motivated by the upward struggle because they were proud of their cultural and religious roots; their self-respect didn't allow them to succumb to pressure even when it meant going through terrible turmoil and leaving behind a life of material comfort to be in abject poverty thereafter. It was their willpower and their self-pride and prowess that made them survive and re-establish themselves. Men and women of these families led the social, familial and, in many instances, personal transformations. They applied their competencies which were connected to a strong sense of identity, pride and the vision of a larger purpose. I belong to this Hindu Brahmin community of Kashmiri Pandits and grew up listening to the tales of uprooting, hardship, and the difficulties faced by a community in exodus and exile.

My grandfather was a self-made man and lived a life of great personal integrity. Our forefathers migrated from Kashmir a number of years ago and my grandfather was brought up in a small township in Madhya Pradesh in central India. As I have mentioned, we are Kashmiri Pandits and even after migration, we retained our Kashmiri habits and traditions. Till the time of my mother's generation, most marriages were within the Kashmiri community. From my generation onwards, a number of marriages have been outside the community. Now, marrying into another community, caste and also religion has become common and acceptable.

At the age of 18, my grandfather left Jaora, the town in Madhya Pradesh where he lived with his parents, and came to Allahabad, Uttar Pradesh, in North India to study law. After completing his degree, he commenced his practice in Allahabad High Court as a criminal lawyer and in the years that followed made a name for himself in the legal profession. In the legal world, he became a force to be reckoned with and as a criminal lawyer, he was known for his sheer brilliance, intellectual clarity, focus and, of course, his intellectual integrity and personal character. He established a very successful legal practice and by the dint of his hard work and professional competence earned very well and was able to build and buy houses and real estate all over North India. My father was the youngest amongst three sons and as a child and even in his early teens grew up in opulence and comfort.

My grandfather also went through a number of personal tragedies. My grandmother got tuberculosis at a very young age and as at that time there was no cure for the disease, she had to be looked after very well and had to lead a more or less secluded life lest the others, especially the children, caught the infection. My father missed the warmth and the physical proximity of his mother as a young child because of her disease and lost her when he was 15.

Apart from losing his wife, my grandfather also lost a young daughter-in-law and a 21-year-old daughter, who perhaps was his favourite child. All these personal losses must have broken him inside but he carried on with his work and official responsibilities.

He joined the Quit India Movement when his practice was at its peak in 1942. He was jailed for a number of years during the independence struggle. After India became independent, his political career commenced and he occupied important political positions in the central cabinet. He held the position of India's law minister, defence minister and home minister. He was also the governor of West Bengal and Odisha and then he became the chief minister of Madhya Pradesh. After losing his elections in Madhya Pradesh in 1962, he returned to Allahabad, stayed with the family and breathed his last on 17 February 1968.

My grandfather did us proud. As a teenager, I had the good fortune of seeing him in office and even after his retirement, when he spent six years with us in Allahabad. What he left behind for the family was immense. I would not like to write about the wealth that he created and passed on to the family. It is far less important than the legacy of national pride, professional reputation, his political ideology and social and familial values which he handed over to all of us. He was a colossus in law and his personal integrity was admirable.

I am blessed to be born to my parents. My father was fundamentally, and in all respects, a spiritual man. He practised as a criminal lawyer in Allahabad

High Court and was elevated to the bench as a judge in 1973. He was known for his sharp intellect, an elephantine memory and his impeccable honesty and uprightness. He was a fearless man. He also served as the chief justice of the Allahabad High Court before his retirement in 1989. Lawyers and judges in the High Court remember him as a man who followed, protected and set the highest standards of legal, judicial and personal integrity.

As a person my father was childlike, loving and contented. He appreciated our achievements, gave us a lot of freedom and also, in his quiet and unobtrusive ways, instilled in us a lot of discipline. I never heard him talk ill of anyone or raise his voice and lose his temper. He had a disarming and a naughty smile and a subtle sense of humour. My mother's mental balance and equanimity and my father's courage were great examples for me which made me pick up the broken pieces of my life and move on after the sudden passing away of my husband in 2002. It was only because of what I had seen in my family and the values that I was able to subconsciously internalise that made me find a credible purpose and my strength to survive, face and manage those difficult years. My son's education and his physical, mental and emotional well-being were my primary purpose to live and work. I had the examples set by my parents to learn from. My pride in them and their character inspired me to live and fight it out.

The power of examples and living through experiences in the family help us learn a lot. In my case, I saw how people faced adversity, fought lonely battles of financial deprivation and through grit, effort and talent bounced back and created their own happiness. Roots can always be struck again even when everything has been uprooted. I learnt many lessons of courage.

3

The Energy Stream

Nothing moves without energy. For good work to happen, power and authority need to be positively energised. Our strong and beautiful bodies cannot move an inch without energy. The powerful engine of a car can't start and the car can't move forward without some litres of petrol.

Leading oneself and others towards continuous improvement or exceptional achievement is all about living with focus and engaging with energy.

I was extremely fortunate to witness the play of such energy many times. It is special and invigorating and one wonders where it comes from. It cannot go unnoticed. It exudes strength and power. There are some leaders who do not seem to tire easily and their eyes sparkle. Even when they are not laughing, a soft smile seems to be playing around their lips indicating happiness, satisfaction and a joyful involvement with life. The energy also electrifies and enlivens the atmosphere around them.

Apart from physical energy, psychological and spiritual energy are also significantly important in life and work. Energy levels have to be built and nurtured. A strong constitution can be a gift of nature but it also depends on genetic endowment, the physical and environmental conditions to which the body is exposed and, of course, the nutrition and other amenities available to the person. It is also seen that when the body is strong, it positively impacts mental and emotional well-being. Leaders can't afford not to look after their physical health as the demands of work and other social engagements on them are heavy and taxing. This is exemplified by leaders involved in sports—for example cricket, which has showcased the energy levels of many leaders who have become captains of the game, having established unprecedented records in sporting history. All stand out for a life of rigid discipline and a focus on physical and psychological health. Brilliant examples are Sachin Tendulkar, Kapil Dev and now Virat Kohli.

Energy is directly connected with health and well-being. Physical health gives us stamina. Psychological health brings us joy and happiness and it can also result in freedom from tension and anxiety and subsequently peace and calm. All these states facilitate mental focus, motivation and engagement with various activities that a person undertakes including those at the workplace. When people lead teams, large or small, or when leaders lead organisations or nations, these qualities help them to perform their roles effectively and efficaciously. It is important to remember that energy and health in its multifarious dimensions contribute immensely and positively to leadership behaviour. The most significant contribution is towards the building of self-confidence and resilience without which leaders will not be able to sustain long hours of work as well as influence teams by their sheer energetic and powerful presence.

The Maestro

I was attending a musical recital in Kolkata in the early eighties. A famous sarod maestro was performing that evening.

However, akin to the great artist who has mastered his art, he played beautifully that evening. The audience was enthralled and he managed to bring them back from their restlessness and impatience. While he played the instrument exquisitely, for about 20 minutes, a leader from the film industry, a world-famous film-maker and director, entered the auditorium. He was not conventionally handsome. I didn't know that he was walking down the aisle towards the front row. I don't know what made me turn to see him. I saw him and for the remaining two hours looked at him many times. I had to. The energy was magnetic. He carried himself with great dignity. Dark, tall and soberly dressed in a pair of jeans and a kurta with a shawl draped around his shoulders, he keenly listened and concentrated on the music. I thought he was enjoying the music, listening with a sense of deep interest and with an uncanny sense of purpose. His energy was purposeful.

He filled the whole auditorium with his presence. Everything faded into the background, including, to a large extent, the recital. I wondered whether this was because of his fame and achievements, or as a result of the energy which he carried with him. I was sure that it was a kind of low, almost subliminal vibration which had pervaded the atmosphere. His energy was pervasive. Was his mental, physical, emotional and spiritual wiring different from us?

The energy was certainly different, intense, purposeful, focused, subtle and infectious. It made many feel energetic and more alive themselves. I could see it during the interval, when he walked out of the auditorium into the lounge and was surrounded immediately by a large group of people who looked happy and joyful interacting with him.

The Gentle Tiger

Let me describe the energy of another leader who was the chairman of a huge multinational company in Kolkata. I worked in that company for a number of years. Whenever I entered the corporate office lobby and he was not around, even without anyone telling me about his absence, I knew that he was not in office that day. The energy in office was very different. The office always felt empty and incomplete in his absence. I found this very strange and it always happened even when the office was full with the rest of the two-hundred people who worked in there.

It is not the physical presence but the mental, emotional and spiritual energy which makes a person's presence felt and experienced. Sometimes, even when the person is absent, his presence is felt. The energy pervades the space and creates a positive difference.

I had entered the lift at the corporate office one Monday afternoon to go to the second floor where the director and the chairman sat. A peon, who had been working in the office for a number of years, was also in the lift. He was an active member of the union and was known for the trouble that he created in the office off and on. He was extremely rude, undisciplined and disrespectful with the senior managers and the directors of the company. Not only that, he was also unpredictable and even rebellious.

As the lift was about to close, the chairman walked into the lift. The peon looked at him with a cocky grin on his face, addressed him by his first name and sarcastically commented on the bad performance of the company that month. I froze out of sheer disbelief and embarrassment and with bated breath awaited an outburst of anger from the chairman.

With my head down, I gazed at the floor of the lift. Nothing happened for a few seconds. I cautiously looked up and saw the chairman extremely calm, composed and smiling. With his hand on the shoulder of the peon and looking straight into his eyes, he greeted him. The peon bent down and touched his feet. The lift stopped on the second floor and the three of us walked out quietly. The chairman asked me if I was enjoying my work. I replied that I was. He gave me a charming smile and walked towards his office.

His energy was awesome, conveying that he could not be disturbed by the negative comment. He expressed empathy through his eyes and touch when he put his hands on the shoulder of the peon. However, his presence was extremely powerful, his authority unmistakable and his anger completely under control. I do not know whether he was angry at all. Smiling genuinely, he asked me about my work. The energy, which could also be described as influence was so overwhelming that in a few seconds, the peon's rebellion vanished as he lowered himself to the floor of the lift to touch the chairman's feet.

The energy of leaders is unique and is of a different quality. It electrifies and enlivens the atmosphere. It is magnetic and pulls people towards itself. The energy is pervasive and does not restrict itself to a small physical space around the leader. It pervades the hearts and the minds of the people. The leader's energy has a purposeful quality. It creates positivity and hope and makes people happy and energetic. The energy also has a calming effect. It is well contained and focused within the leader, is infectious and is abundant and overflowing all the time.

Willing to Go on

Here is another story. I have kept the name of the company and that of the manager anonymous.

The human resources (HR) department of the company was always under pressure for good performance as it reported directly to the chairman of the company. The chairman believed that the HR function was the backbone of the business and had to be fully and always aware of people and business issues. He believed that human potential was the invaluable asset of the company and personally took a lot of interest in the development of people, including the workforce, in all the seven manufacturing facilities in India.

The chairman, it was known throughout the organisation, had never cancelled or missed a single meeting on HR, despite his constant travel throughout India and overseas. One Monday morning, the head of HR reached office two hours before time to complete the preparations for an annual performance review of the corporate HR team.

The agenda for the meeting was circulated a week in advance. The chairman was in Europe and had only returned the night before. The HR head came to know that the chairman's aircraft had landed well past midnight and the HR review was to commence at 9 AM on Monday. They wondered whether the chairman had the time to read the agenda. If not, how would they take him through the presentation on their work for that year?

The chairman hardly lost his temper and was never irritable. However, as his days were normally loaded with work, he hated delays in meetings, not finishing the meeting on time and people not being prepared for meetings.

The chairman walked into the boardroom at five minutes to nine, looking relaxed. The HR head began to shuffle some papers in sheer nervousness as the chairman walked briskly towards him. He wished him softly, convinced that the chairman was bound to tell him that the agendas for such important reviews should be sent two weeks in advance and HR should check his travel schedule before planning for meetings where his presence is required.

As he brushed passed the HR team he turned around, and with a mischievous smile said, 'Why do you make this old man work so hard? I finished reading your agenda at 3 AM and here it is, I've made my notes.' The HR head quickly flipped through the pages. In the tiniest handwriting, the chairman had written his observations along every paragraph of the document. No one could fathom where he drew this abundant energy from.

What could be the secret behind the energy that leaders display? The time I spent with these leaders from corporate organisations and also my understanding of the experiences of my colleagues has convinced me of a few reasons. The energy of leaders emanates from the dreams that they nurture in their minds and hearts. It is contained in the purpose for which they live and work. It flourishes and expands in the freedom that they give to their minds to absorb different ideas and experiences. Their positivity is energising and empowering. The source of energy is their willpower. They keep replenishing their energy by spending it in great work. The satisfaction that they derive from such work replenishes their energy faster than it is expended. A strong, unbendable, unbreakable will appears to be the secret source of this energy.

As a result of high energy, leaders work for longer hours and also utilise their time more productively. I have found many leaders multi-task, thereby handling different types of work at the same time. They know how to introduce variety into the work for breaking monotony. However, everyone can't multi-task as this requires the ability to move from one task to another seamlessly and also focus on diverse activities. It does require a higher level of energy altogether.

I know a lady, a senior leader in a company, who can complete five to seven different and complex tasks in an hour. She is ready with solutions to solve complex union-related problems in a factory and simultaneously discuss the menu for a company dinner with her secretary as well as check the ingredients of a continental dish with the corporate chef of a five-star hotel chain. In the midst of all this I have heard her dictate off a sensitive and complex report on performance feedback for one senior director reporting to her. I was amazed to see the details that she remembered and her meticulous planning of the report structure. She had really prepared well. Moreover, she remembered a number of examples which corroborated her assessment. I admired her memory. It must be kept in mind that a good recall and recollection is also largely dependent on the interest in remembering and using your memory which is strengthened through rehearsal and practice. The more we use a muscle the stronger it becomes. In this case the brain muscle becomes stronger by using it more. The memory channels in the brain deepen, making recall and recollection easier.

The energy levels in the family, organisation or in society also depict the productive contribution of leadership competencies towards enhancing motivation and inspiration. When people lead well, the work atmosphere in organisations is energised positively and there is a general feeling of well-being and joy. Similarly in a family when parents and elders lead well and keep building the self-confidence and motivation of their children, there is a perceptible cheer and positivity in the family atmosphere. One litmus test of such a family atmosphere is the number of people and friends who visit the family. Such happy families attract people and opportunities. In these families, because of the presence of role models, good leadership, coaching and mentoring the younger generation also imbibes leadership qualities and behaviours.

High energy levels are also good indicators of high resilience, which is the capacity to cope with stress and difficulty and recover quickly. Resilient people don't succumb to pressure easily and have the quality to convert a distressing situation into an opportunity. This tendency facilitates the attainment of stretched targets and helps in realising hidden talent and potential. Leaders who are resilient themselves build this capacity in the team. Resilience also helps in coping with prolonged periods of tension and helps in working under pressure. Leaders who have this trait do an excellent job of execution and implementation because it requires the ability to manage pressure so as to attain targets. Operational leaders, those who lead functions like production or sales, or in other words, such business activities on the ground, display such competencies and skills. Their high energy levels go a long way in providing the stamina for arduous and continuous travel. It also helps them interact with the frontline when troubleshooting.

A strong will therefore, appears to be a significant game changer for leaders as it not only provides high energy levels for persistent hard work but also strengthens resilience. When plans are translated into action on the ground it is normal for leaders and their teams to encounter unforeseen problems and hurdles. The will to persist and forge ahead helps in a big way. This together with smart thinking and multitasking are unmistakably effective competencies of leaders for managing successful implementation of plans and strategies.

4

The Wheel of Time

Respect for time is respect for life and its possibilities. Those who respect time are those who respond well and assume responsibility.

Leaders have a special relationship with time. Those that I came into contact with treated time with great respect. They hated wasting time—their own and that of others. They were acutely conscious of the fact that time was limited and, therefore, very precious. Surprisingly, they never said that they did not have sufficient time to handle things that were of importance. They also found time for their interests and hobbies as well as for family and friends.

Time is usually not considered a resource to be utilised well. We take time for granted. Often we don't realise that time is like any other resource and much more. Whoever has succeeded in the world has been able to do so because one of the many other things that the person has managed well is time. Doing more in a lesser amount of time, doing things at the right time, doing many different things in the same time, keeping time utilisation and management plans ready for the future and utilising every minute productively is the hallmark of a great leader. People have different perspectives on time and they relate with time differently. For some, time is perceived as a schedule and framework for activities and for others it is fluid, in larger segments or chunks of mornings, afternoons, evenings and nights. For some, the afternoon commences at 12 PM and for others, afternoons only commence at 2 PM. Some people call themselves morning people as they are most active and perhaps in a happier and lighter mental frame in the mornings and some are afternoon types as they are most active and energetic in the afternoon and can put in a lot of work then. Some are early birds and some work best after 12 AM and can stay awake throughout the night. We also have biorhythms worked out today which tell us which time of the day and which day in the week will be the best for us physically, emotionally and mentally so that we can plan our work and other activities accordingly. The best time is worked out according to our positive energy levels. However, our bodies and mind keep emitting signals regularly which make us aware of our best energy patterns according to daily time frames during which our positive energies actually peak.

Similarly, we have a pattern or trend about spending our life mentally in the past, present or the future. Some of us have a stronger pull towards the past. This pull makes us live more in the past mentally, in our childhood, in the time that has been, in happier times of the past and even in the mistakes, regrets, fears and guilt of the past. This attraction to the past could also take us to the study of history, anthropology and culture. We could also be fascinated with old stamps, museums, and even by the study of the evolution of the universe, certain aspects of astronomy and astrology and to many other things connected with the past.

Some of us live mentally more in the future through our day—dreams, aspirations, ambitions and even our dissatisfaction and disappointment of the past and present. Some work hard to improve the future while others don't and only dream or fret about it. Being too preoccupied with the future could make us fearful, anxious, impractical and unrealistic and even delusional. If we are attracted strongly to the future we might choose to dabble in future studies which cover strategic thinking, future scenario planning, technology and sciences for innovation, and methodologies for predicting future trends, or even prepare ourselves professionally to manage the future of our work and careers much better. There are in fact universities and institutes today which are solely dedicated to the study of the future more through research in innovation, evolution of species and historical and universal events, and other creative pursuits.

There are very few of us who are mindfully engaged with the present. Mindfulness ensures complete focus and attention to what we are involved with as well as enjoyment of what we are doing. For example, if we are combing our hair, then giving complete attention to combing ensures mindfulness. We should be paying attention to all the details and enjoying every second of the activity. When we tell ourselves that we don't like combing our hair we are in the same breadth saying that we don't like our hair and that combing and looking after our hair is not important. We also say that we don't believe that our hair will make any difference to our physical appearance or health. When we understand the meaning of this, only then will we appreciate the importance of combing and this will change our attitude and bring more mindfulness to the act of combing itself. Therefore valuing all that we have in the present will also increase our mindfulness. Gratitude for things that we have and not to constantly worry and hanker for things that we don't have make us focus more in the present than the past or the future. Our awareness that the past has gone away and left us never to return, and the future has yet to happen, will make us live more in the present than we normally do, be mindful in it, feel grateful for all its gifts and enjoy them. It is worthwhile to remember that everything happens in the present. Therefore not to value it is the greatest folly that any human being can commit. Most of us commit this mistake and in doing so attract and live in misery.

Each person relates with time in his or her way and has a unique way of managing it. People don't think of time in identical ways because some are more concerned with the time that has passed and some keep waiting for the time which is yet to come. Some have a more planned and structured approach to time and some feel comfortable with just flowing into large chunks of the 24 hours as morning, evening, afternoon and night. Some are able to do a lot in less time and some have just one thing to do and therefore time could just hang on. Some don't know what to do because 24 hours seem to be very long while some don't know where it goes and wish that each day were of 40 hours, and even then, they would be short of time. However, most leaders do some common things with time. They value time, manage it well in their own unique style and don't feel good about wasting it.

The Magic of Time Skills

This leader whom I am writing about was an extremely busy managing director of a huge multinational company headquartered in Mumbai. He was known for his personal discipline and his sense of time. He never wore a wrist watch. Mobiles had not entered the Indian market in the late seventies. He never failed once in his estimation and perception of the exact time during any part of the day.

At 1 PM sharp, he would get up for lunch and start walking towards the cafeteria. Just watching the sun go down, he would announce to the board room that the discussion could on for another 15 minutes only, and that much time was left to wrap up, before six in the evening. He would proudly say that the exact time was 4.35 PM. His team members looked at their wrist watches to find that he was shockingly correct. This happened many times. People found this uncanny and mysterious. Many people believed it to be a gift with which he was born. Some felt that his discipline helped him to develop this skill.

Leaders are acutely aware of time. They also know how to integrate the past, the present and the future. They use the processes and knowledge emanating from experience, learning and planning to do this. They normally ask questions like:

1. What have your experiences in the past taught you which you can apply to solve your problems today or not allow such problems to occur at all in the future?
2. Can you introspect or journey into the past to learn from your past successes and failures?
3. Based on your past experiences and what is happening in the present, can you visualise the future and plan and prepare yourself to face it effectively?
4. At the end of each day leaders who manage their time efficiently and effectively ask themselves whether they have, in fact, utilised the entire day well. They value every minute of the day and keep improving their skills for managing it.

Making Your Mark

Another 80-year-old owner and chairman of a company is in office before time. As a young man he migrated to Amritsar as a refugee from Lahore which is now in Pakistan. His family lost all the property and wealth during the partition of India and Pakistan. His family was lucky to receive financial help from the Indian government for rehabilitation. His father got a job with the state government in the Punjab. With some security and money coming to the family again the owner-chairman could join college to complete his graduation. He then started working in an ordnance factory run by the Indian army in central India. The youngest of four brothers, he was very attached to his parents who felt happy that he had a secure job.

Missing his parents and home and not liking the routine aspect of the work in the factory, he packed his bags and resigned from the job. Even though his parents were happy to have him back in the house, they were quite concerned about his impulsive behaviour and the fact that he would not be meaningfully engaged during the day.

Sleeping at night had become rare for him because he made plans to do something on his own and thought a lot about the future in the silent dark hours when he was alone in his room. Twenty-four years old, he set out to take charge of his life. He was fully aware about the transience of things because he had witnessed everything destroyed in front of his eyes when the family fled from Lahore during the partition. Nothing stays, time does not wait and no one can predict what can happen in the next moment. Do not wait, start it now, his heart told him and he did. The money that he had saved from his job in the ordnance factory helped him to set up a small timber-cutting workshop. The garage of a friendly neighbour was converted into the workshop.

After that, there was no looking back for him. The timber business grew, which he sold off to buy a small factory manufacturing switches. As the years rolled on, he added on a number of factories and products which grew by leaps and bounds into a huge business empire. His sense of timing for decisions was perfect.

These stories show that leaders relate to time in a special way. They have an instinct and an awareness about time and can sense and estimate it accurately helping them to utilise that time to their advantage. They have a knack of knitting together the past, the present and the future. This integration helps them to learn, plan, sustain as well as innovate themselves and their role and work.

Leaders hate wasting time and display a sense of urgency. They achieve more in less time. They are punctual and do not make others wait, they respect others' time as well. They can correctly apportion time for various activities that make them productive. In this way their relating to time well helps them plan effectively. It also allows them time their decisions perfectly.

The Time Wizard

An institute of management in Kolkata decided to conduct a study on time management. There was a very senior leader in an industry based in Kolkata known for his exceptional skills in time management. I was given the task to contact and set up a discussion meeting with him and the professors and research associates.

I met the senior leader and requested him to give us an hour for the meeting. He said, 'Why do you require an hour?' I didn't know what to say and fumbled and responded tentatively, 'Okay sir . . . may be 45 minutes will do.' The reply was, 'Why 45 minutes? Why not 43?' This completely stumped me and then I heard him say that he would be available for 43 minutes. Not knowing how to respond, I thanked him and left his office.

We reached his office well in time. At 10 AM on the dot, we were ushered in. He was so well-prepared for the discussion that it was truly amazing. We were all really impressed with his responses to the questions from the team. We were so involved with the discussion that we forgot about the time and winding up the meeting. However, he didn't forget and managed to skilfully wrap up the meeting. It was 10.43. Not once did he mention time or appeared to be under pressure. The research team left his office speechless, totally impressed with his amazing skill and artistry with managing time. Our lessons from the manner in which leaders relate to and manage time were deep and insightful.

Leaders who have respect and an understanding of work and responsibility display a continuous respect for time. Not only do they have sufficient time for work and to pursue their interests, but they also have an acute awareness of time and display amazing skills to integrate the past, present and future. They time their work and decisions very effectively and possess the skills to negotiate for time. Preparing well on the time management front also means that they meet their timelines and targets.

5

Unspoken Pain

There are many languages of pain and it is expressed in a variety of ways, through tears and laughter, silence and chatter, and sleep and toil. It is understood more by the heart than the mind.

What has pain got to do with leadership? Most leaders I interacted with shared that they had experienced immense psychological pain in their lives. Some had gone through pain in their childhood and some later. The pain was because of rejection, frustration, guilt, humiliation, loneliness or low self-worth.

The psychology of pain is significantly important to understand. Pain creates physical, mental and emotional discomfort. It may last for a little time or it could linger on indefinitely. We could be very bad in managing it and, therefore, keep complaining about it, cry in pain or even become immobilised by pain.

Mental pain is largely a result of frustration and disappointment. It can also be caused by a feeling of being let down and losing faith and trust. Sudden events cause pain because of the accompanying uncertainty and ambiguity. These conditions make many people uncomfortable and insecure. The underlying fear, insecurity and unpredictability can cause pain, confusion and conflict. Mental pain results from facing situations which we don't understand too well and are completely unequipped to handle them. Loss of a near and dear member of the family causes mental agony and emotional distress. In fact most of the time there is a thin line of demarcation between mental and emotional pain and both appear to be closely connected.

Emotional distress is usually a combination of feelings of sorrow, depression and anxiety. It is caused by going through loss, separation from people, places and or illnesses, leaving the person weak and helpless. It is also a result of being resource deprived and therefore feeling like life is full of struggle and strife, bringing worry and anxiety, feelings of low self-worth and self-esteem. Poverty is one of the main causes of emotional distress or pain.

Downside Up

Polio struck him when he was a two-year-old toddler. He developed a bad limp and could never participate in sports in school. He always felt left out and some of his classmates were cruel and had nicknamed him *langda* or crippled. As he grew older, his friend circle shrunk because of his inability to ride a cycle or a scooter and so, he could not socialise with friends in the evenings. He lost out on a lot of fun. Being often alone in the evenings, he found time to read and started enjoying it. Whenever he had spare money he would buy books and would also encourage his siblings to read. Interestingly, his grandmother was an educated and versatile woman and read almost all the books that he bought or issued from the college library. He topped the B.Com examination and decided to pursue chartered accountancy. There were financial problems at home. Two sisters had to be married and his mother's health was gradually failing. Being the only son, he felt responsible and began to supplement the family income by taking tuitions.

He cleared his chartered accountancy exam in the first attempt and obtained exceptionally good grades in all the papers. Three months had passed since he had commenced his apprenticeship in a chartered accounting firm in Kolkata when he received an offer for a job from a multinational company in the accounts department.

He intuitively knew that God and his good luck were responsible for the excellent opportunity that he had obtained. If he worked hard, he believed that there would be no need of looking back. It was just so. He rapidly rose in the accounts and finance department and became known for his depth of knowledge, capacity to work extremely hard, indefatigable energy, good management skills and his understanding of the business and the industry.

The organisation proactively invested in his development, nominating him to management courses all over the world. He had his share of problems and challenges both at home and at work. However, his grit and determination were amazing. He had launched a psychological war against polio from his childhood. The pain of being physically handicapped propelled him to become mentally and emotionally strong. He did not succumb to the disability and putting the anxiety behind him rose to become the first chairman of the company who had a finance background. All his predecessors were all from sales and marketing, and had travelled the length and breadth of the country. He couldn't travel much because of the problem with his legs but he was knowledgeable and sensitive.

How does pain contribute in the development of leadership qualities? Leaders realise early in life that no one else can share one's pain and in the final analysis it has to be borne and managed by the person himself. The experience of pain is personal. Since it is experienced by the individual, it is only the individual who can lessen it for himself and also for those around him. The person has to take responsibility to do something about it. Pain, therefore, helps in developing responsibility. If pain has to be endured, then the other areas of happiness have to be actively pursued and the person has to search for additional personal sources of strength. It is also important to identify personal and professional strengths that can help in managing pain. Pain could also be experienced as a challenge for survival, both physical and emotional. Individuals learn a plethora of compensatory behaviours to manage and relieve pain. Challenges to self-worth, confidence and self-respect are also accepted during emotionally and physically painful experiences. Pain appears to fuel grit, determination, will-power and courage. Such experiences have helped focus on developing expertise, skills and support systems.

Rejection to Resilience

He was only 18 years old when he experienced trauma and humiliation. During a wedding in the family, he met a girl his age and fell in love with her. He waited for a few months and when he was sure that it was love and not infatuation, he sent a marriage proposal to her parents. The girl belonged to a well-to-do and a very well-placed family. She was beautiful and educated. He was overweight, not good-looking and without a job. However, he was extremely intelligent and sharp. His father was an ordinary government officer and because of the difference in the families' status he did not have the courage to pursue the matter with the girl's family. Ironically, the girl had developed a soft corner for him and somehow he came to know this from a close friend.

The girl's family completely disapproved of the marriage proposal. This news reached him through a friend. He felt deeply hurt when he heard the negative comments made by the girl's family on his middle class family background. Their comments on his ordinary looks and their lack of confidence in his ability to do well, he thought, were completely uncalled for. He took this rather maturely but a friend who was very close to him understood his anguish and anger. On a cold December night, after a year since the rejection he boarded a ship and sailed to the United Kingdom (UK). He had borrowed some money from a relative and assured him that he would begin to repay the loan as soon as he got a job on the completion of his post-graduation from the London School of Economics (LSE). He topped his batch in LSE and on returning to India, joined a reputed multinational company. As promised, he began to pay off the loan. The girl whom he had loved and who had waited for him became his wife and he rose to become one of the most admired, loved and successful corporate leaders that the country has known. He related this story to those who were close to him. He believed that but for the pain at the age of 18, he would not have achieved what he did. The initial rejection that he faced helped him to become resilient and determined.

Most of us experience rejection sometimes in our lives. We can feel rejected by our parents, spouses or friends. Rejection normally results in us feeling humiliated and small. Humiliation is hurting for the dignity, and the self-respect of an individual is hurt. Self-respect and dignity are valued by people. Even the poorest of the poor value their dignity and self-respect and don't take attempts to hurt it lying down. These are instances which are rarely forgotten by people and the resultant pain and hurt can be remembered and harboured for years. Relationships, very often, sour because of such experiences. Ultimately, people who hurt the self-respect and dignity of others also lose respect in the eyes of those whom they hurt.

Resurrection

Here is another story. He was a middle-level manager working with a company in Andhra Pradesh which exported shrimps to Japan and South East Asia. Being in internal audit he had to travel to the small factories and the company offices along the east coast of the state. The corporate office was in Guntur, a fairly big city and an educational centre. The family shifted from the village and joined him and the children joined a convent school and were happily settled. The daughter was very attached to him. She was a talented and a sensitive child and was growing up well as a twelve-year-old.

The summer vacations for the children had arrived and they wanted a short trip outside Guntur. He thought that the best thing would be to take the family with him on his next official tour to Vishakhapatnam. He booked rooms in a lovely hotel which overlooked the beach and planned to fly with the family to the location. It was an early morning flight and they landed on time. Summer temperatures were very high there and he, therefore, arranged for an air-conditioned spacious taxi from the airport to the hotel.

The hotel was about 40 kilometres from the airport. The driver was cautious and drove very sensibly. He was happy to see the children excited, chirpy and bright like the strong sun which shone on the sea along the coast. Their mother had a smile on her face, looked relaxed and, as usual, was her calm and poised self.

He had picked up a newspaper from the airport and had begun to read it. He found the space at the front a little cramped and exchanged the front seat near the driver with his daughter and shifted to the back on her insistence. She wanted to sit in front.

There was a big explosion. He didn't have the time to think as he completely blanked out. The car had collided head-on with a truck and then, losing balance, skidded on the road and hit a tree. He regained consciousness to hear the loud uncontrollable wailing of his wife. His daughter had died on the spot and the son was in a critical condition. The daughter was declared dead on being taken to the hospital. His son had fractured a number of bones. He, his wife and the driver escaped the fatal accident with minor scratches.

A month later, sipping his cup of coffee, he thought of resuming work. He still felt numb with sorrow and pain but had to put up a brave front for his wife, his old mother and the son who had been discharged from the hospital and was convalescing at home. The emotional wound was too deep. No amount of sympathy and support from relatives and friends was helping. He didn't want to go on anti-depressants and was determined to fight it out. He was clear in his mind that he couldn't crack under any pressure because of the responsibility of the family. His son was still a child and had his entire life in front of him.

One evening, driving home from office, he stopped at the university and obtained admission in an evening two-year course on business administration. He diligently pursued the course and completed it in time. He was also doing well at work. He completed a specialised diploma in HR. News spread in the company regarding his exceptional contribution in audit and he was thereafter promoted and transferred to finance. He immersed himself in work, actively guided his son who began to achieve excellent results and having topped in his board exam, secured admission in the Indian Institute of Technology (IIT) at Mumbai. Encouraged by him, his wife began teaching in a school and joined a ladies club which organised vocational training for destitute women. The family also started a scholarship in the name of their daughter.

He and his son were doing outstandingly well in their respective careers. After a decade and a half he was promoted to the company board as a deputy chairman and in his speech to the members in the corporate office he said, 'My daughter is 25 now. She lives in my heart and is with me. I know that she is very happy today and knew what I was capable of doing. She has contributed hugely in my success by giving me the strength to live without her physical presence. Today I speak with immense conviction that our near and dear ones are always with us.' He became one of the most admired leaders of the company.

Accepting the tragic blows of life requires immense courage. Acceptance comes from understanding the logic of things. Realistically, there are many things that we cannot control and cannot find answers to explain why they occur. Therefore, it is best that we accept things as they come and do it with stoic dignity and responsibility. There are some joys in life that come unexpectedly and we accept them. We have to do the same with pain that comes with inexplicable and sudden happenings. Acceptance matures us and frees our mind and spirit to engage with things that we can influence and manage. Leaders have an uncanny aptitude to do this and do it successfully.

The Turning of the Page

Pain can become a roadblock. How do leaders get propelled to manage life and become successful despite the pain? What insights accrue from pain? How does it fuel achievement and what are the challenges that it brings in its wake? How does it help shape self, identity and role? How are the hurt and emotional distress altered for leading us to take responsibility for results and for life as a whole? These are important questions to be answered and there are so many stories of leaders who have managed pain quietly and have not stopped contributing to others and taking life as it comes. Very often leaders hold life by the horns and take it head-on.

She lived in a remote village in Rajasthan, a state on the western borders of India. Rajasthan has one of the largest deserts in Asia, sprinkled with far-flung villages without fertile land and water. The village folk encounter a tough life on a day-to-day basis because of this. With no educational and medical facilities in the villages, in the desert along the India–Pakistan border, parents do not hope for a bright future for their children. Water and medical aid are constant concerns. People are used to witnessing patients succumbing to death from diseases which today can be controlled with early medical attention and care.

They were quite well-off when her husband was alive. Her husband earned from the camel which they owned by selling camel milk and employing the animal for the transportation requirements of the village community. She could make blue pottery, which was a special craft of the state. She was attached to a family manufacturing pottery on a large scale and took orders from them on a monthly basis for designing and painting before the pottery was sent to be baked. She was also keen on learning stitching and sewing because of her interest in design and colours.

Then one afternoon, tragedy struck. Her husband, in the heat of a summer afternoon, suffered a massive stroke which left him completely paralysed neck downwards. They didn't have enough money for his medication and after three months, perhaps as a result of uncontrolled blood pressure, he passed away from what appeared to be a cardiac arrest. Left with three children, two daughters and a son, with no money or support from the family, she was broken in spirit and extremely anxious about the future. She sold off the camel to get money to meet the daily needs of the family. There were also debts to be paid which she had taken for the medical treatment of her late husband.

I met her three years ago in her village which I visited when the organisation in which I work decided to inaugurate a community development project in that area. When I met her, she was running a very successful sewing school which made her earn about ₹10,000 a month—the kind of money which the family had never seen before. She could also afford to send her daughters to school.

How did this happen? Three months after her husband passed away, and surviving with the money that came to her from the sale of the camel, she lost her only son. Burning up with high temperature, her son died in her arms when she was taking him to a primary health centre in a neighbouring village. The village community blamed her for not looking after him. They blamed her inauspicious stars which inflicted tragedy on the family. When she did not shed a single tear on her son's death, the village community described her as a weird, heartless mother. She was determined to do something with her life and didn't want her daughters to see and experience what she had. She took training for six months and set up the sewing school all by herself. She instilled self-confidence and positivity in her daughters. Three years ago when I met her and listened to her story, she put her head in my lap and wailed uncontrollably. I felt very proud of her. What a human being! What a mother and what great leadership in unimaginable adversity!

6

Mindset Matters

A positively set and well-tuned-in mind is like the TV antenna which catches all the signals and is set to enable a clear, focused and enlightened view of the world.

Like the TV antenna, which has to be set to catch the signal, or the correct installation of the tower that facilitates the network needed for a mobile phone, the setting and the tuning of the mind is required for functioning well in any given context. Human, social and business settings are varied. The contexts in which the mind functions today are dynamic and complex. The design of the mind, its setting or the configuration, depends on beliefs, values, assumptions, memories, knowledge, information, perceptions and the feelings of the person. The mindset influences the person's reactions, responses and behaviours towards people, work and situations. If a person is born and brought up in a small town and then shifts to a metropolitan city, he or she takes time to adjust because the person has a 'small town mindset'. This simply means that small towns and big cities have a different social, economic and professional culture and ethos. Lifestyles are different in small and big cities and managing day-to-day life could require different arrangements and competencies. Small-town thinking could be more traditional and big town more cosmopolitan and modern. This does not mean that one is good and the other is bad. The mindsets created are just different.

Leaders are found in small and big towns. Leaders are not only the CEOs of organisations, ministers in the government or people who have achieved high and well in their professions. A homemaker can play a leadership role in her family most effectively and a worker in a factory can be an admired leader of his team. Similarly, a farmer in a village can be an effective leader in his community. It is also a complex setting but its complexity is rural and traditional and not urban and cosmopolitan.

Can we say that there is a 'leadership mindset' which facilitates a leader to respond in a special or a different way in whichever setting in which he or she leads?

My belief is that a leader's mindset is oriented or tuned towards people. Leading fundamentally means showing a future direction and facilitating a journey along that direction with other people. Leaders cannot lead machines or materials. Therefore leadership necessarily is about setting future directions for people and journeying with those people along that direction. The leader's mindset focuses on shared-goals. An example could be when a farmer leader mobilises support from within the community members to build a school for the children of the village. Understanding problems and identifying solutions is also a characteristic of a leader's mindset. A leader's mindset is tuned to managing contradictions such as the short and the long-term goals, security and risk, status quo as well as change, traditions and modernity. It works best for co-creating solutions and uses the strength of others for this. It understands influence and power and can use it effectively and positively to obtain a win-win outcome. It is result-focused. It can create and sustain varied and complex relationships. The mindset is tuned for spotting and utilising big and small opportunities. There is an inspirational quality in the mindset.

The Entrepreneur as a Leader

He was born in a tiny village in North India which was bereft of electricity, a good-quality school, a primary health centre and clean drinking water. Having lost his mother at the age of 16 and being the eldest among four brothers, he had to assume a number of motherly responsibilities for his younger siblings. Cooking became a daily chore and so did cleaning and obtaining water from the nearby well.

Being a brilliant student, he managed to reach high school despite the workload and the emotional strain at home and was determined to do well in the school examinations. He aspired for college education and later applied for a scholarship which took him to USA for higher studies. His efforts and hard work did not go to waste. Having topped the high school examination, he secured admission in one of the best colleges in Delhi for a bachelor's degree in political science. Incidentally he became the first person to clear the high school examination from his village. The community was very proud of his achievements.

After his graduation, he went through a rough patch when he suffered a dreadful attack of small pox which made him lose all vision in his left eye. Psychologically, he was shattered and lost a lot of his self-confidence. However, being a determined man, he marched ahead and obtained a scholarship for a postgraduate degree in political science from USA and returned to India after his doctorate in the same subject.

Evidently, his mind was set to explore new areas and influence his family elders who were traditional grain traders to allow him to study. This was a major change which the family managed rather well. He set the trend for his younger brothers who also developed academic interests and obtained degrees in engineering and business administration.

When he returned from USA with an American wife, it created a major furore in the community. Fortunately the lady had a sweet temperament and won over his family, relatives and friends. She turned out to be an extremely understanding wife. With her support and encouragement he progressed in his career rapidly and became the head of the department in a reputed college of management and also became an advisor to a number of companies.

Later, he led the movement in these companies for a scientific and professional system of goal and target setting and working on long term strategic plans. It did not take him time to rise to dizzy heights as a business management consultant. He mentored managing directors and chairmen of many organisations and led his consulting work from the position of respect for his expertise, intellectual integrity and brilliance.

His entrepreneurial mindset spotted consulting opportunities in India and overseas. With his flair for influencing and networking at the highest levels with the government and the corporate sector, he was able to establish a centre for learning which is still running extremely well. This is a story of a young boy who managed to develop a modern and professional mindset, different from the traditional, agrarian and feudal environment in which he was brought up till his teens. He led his life and work aided by a mindset which assisted him to explore and influence those around him. He inspired a number of students, professional managers and captains of several industries.

Very simply put, a mindset can also be defined as a habitual way of thinking. It is said that habits die hard and by and large it is true. It is easier to change mindsets when we are young. Exposure to new surroundings and ideas and experience can alter our mindset. However, as we grow older our mental habits become rigid and it is difficult to change these habits in later years. Sometimes a sudden and a tragic event might jolt us out of our mental habits. However, this may not happen with everyone and more often than not even when the mental habits shift, it is temporary. There are many examples which indicate that people who have the potential to lead display a more complex and pliable mindset than those who don't have this propensity. Responding to the context and to opportunities with alacrity and influence, and taking advantage of emerging possibilities with the required mental agility and flexibility are very often displayed by leaders.

Living on Her Own Terms

Here is a story of a woman who had a very different mindset from the family in which she was born and bred. With her mindset she managed to live on her own terms. She wanted to make something of her life. She was a very good student and because of her academic achievements managed a job in a reputed multinational company in Mumbai. Living alone in the metropolis taught her many things. She developed confidence to be independent and to manage the minor challenges of daily living. Standing in the que to pay the electricity bill or organising a plumber for a leaking tap were not difficult chores anymore. Even handling a rude and unfair senior was not a major strain. Stretched sales targets were achieved with ease as she accepted that success does not come easily to anyone and enjoying work also entails accepting the competitive nature of corporate battles.

A long stint in Mumbai and accelerated rise on the corporate ladder brought her work satisfaction and organisational accolades but left her lonely and hankering for companionship and emotional security. As luck would have it she met this very interesting, erudite and a rather unconventional and blaze young man at a company dinner. They kept in touch for almost two years and then decided to marry.

Marriage was not an easy ride at all. She had to take care of a large conservative family, and had an unending list of social obligations and expectations that she had to fulfil. She also had to devote time to a growing son and her own company which she had established. After marriage, she decided to give up her job and jumped at a partnership with a dear friend into the business of over-the-counter Mughlai food sale. It was a small arrangement but was being talked about for the food quality and quick service.

Tragedy has a way of stealthily wriggling its way in, particularly when things begin to look upwards and life is not too bad. One winter morning, in fact when dawn was about to break, her world became as dark as ever. Her husband met with a fatal road accident and passed away. For a week, she was numb and kept observing her teenage son who looked lost and had withdrawn into himself.

It was the quietest night that she had ever spent. All the relatives left for their homes and understandably so, because life had to go on. Yes, she thought, her life has to go on too. And it did move on. It took her four months to find a job in China through a friend who had settled there with her family. Despite strong opposition from her family and relatives she shifted with her son to China, determined to explore the new opportunity and rebuild a home for the child who had grown up overnight as a result of the irreparable personal loss. It's been 20 years since she moved to Shanghai. The happiest moment for her recently was when her son, now a married businessman, told her 'Ma, you made the right decision and responded to our difficulties with much grace, gratitude and grit.' She led her life on her own terms.

7

Results Resonate

Results mirror the reasons for living and working. They are the milestones that measure, judge and reward the journey. The larger purpose thus gets translated into visible outcomes.

What about results? Leaders work for results. They are unforgiving and ruthless with themselves and with others if results are not obtained.

They work for results which are difficult and yet possible to achieve. Their oral and written communication is a lot about results, targets, goals, outcomes, performance levels and bench marks .They get inspired and motivated with results. Professional business leaders look for results in many areas:

1. Achieving better profits and margins
2. Enhanced quality of products and processes
3. Foolproof systems, processes and procedures
4. People with great competencies and talent
5. Organisational reputation, image, brand and goodwill
6. Short and long-term results focus

Leaders wish for the performance bar to keep rising. They have a need to compare results against benchmarks and best practices. Leaders like to stringently monitor performances against set targets and reviews of performances are data-based. With single-minded focus, they work on results. Leaders encourage multi-skilling and multi-tasking in order to enhance performance. They are not only impressed with hard work but also with smart work and they always admire the ability to solve complex and difficult problems that are encountered during work for results. Leaders also appreciate it when individuals and teams take accountability for results. They can be punitive and ruthless if results are not achieved.

Effulgent Effort

He was the chairman of a public sector giant in India. The organisation was going through immense problems when he took charge. There were intense industrial relations issues as the organisation's five huge plants were all located in eastern India and were constantly impacted, for a number of decades, by a volatile leftist political regime.

The organisation's performance was dipping every month and it was running at a loss. The board of the company was answering tough questions in parliament as its role in the development of infrastructure in the country could not be underestimated. A new name for the chairman's role had been proposed and a clearance from the ministry and the cabinet was awaited. The previous appointments of chairmen had always been political.

His name was cleared by the cabinet and he took charge as the new chairman of the company. With an excellent track record, he was widely known for his trouble shooting capabilities and effectively leading organisational turn-arounds.

The unions were extremely hostile, the workforce was by and large indolent, and the supervisors and managers disengaged. The quality of products and processes was getting a beating and the rapid decrease in productivity and profitability were becoming alarming concerns. He was completely aware of the problems and their major causes. After leading a number of discussions with his senior leadership team he concluded that the leadership process in the organisation required direction and focus and leaders had to get more engaged with people right across all levels, functions and locations.

He personally led the process and attended every training programme in the management development institute of the organisation. He was personally present and conducted training sessions and meetings for the improvement in the overall quality and setting of key performance areas at all hierarchical levels and functions. A very tight pressure on results was maintained for six months. The fact that he personally led this made a difference and the performance of the organisation started demonstrating an upward swing. After a year the organisation came out of the loss situation and a few years later showed profits. It was a great day for him as it reaffirmed his belief that a leader should never lose focus from results. He believed that leaders must set personal examples and also lead from the front.

What can we learn from this story?

1. Achieving results for leaders is important.
2. Leaders display high levels of commitment, determination, and engagement.
3. They also have the ability to connect with employees at all levels.
4. Some leaders display the ability to manage power and the external environment exceptionally well.

5. Leaders drive results through people and most times lead from the front.
6. Leaders use communication and conversation as effective ways of influencing and motivating the team.
7. Leaders provide clarity of direction and focus and play a supportive and a facilitative role.

Transformation and change management in organisations is not an easy task. In fact, managing transformation anywhere and at all times has always been challenging. Leaders have to meet and surmount resistance inside the organisation as well as from outside, from external stakeholders. There is the fear of risk and uncertainty and loss of control which vested parties might apprehend. The balance of power and authority in organisations becomes disturbed and this itself is difficult to accept and handle. Moreover, when old practices are disturbed, and new ones take time to be accepted and applied, there are delays in completing work and achieving set targets. This is not easy for leaders to manage and they might face blame and disapproval. It requires immense self-confidence and determination to sail through the initial turmoil of transformation and subsequently scale new heights in results, process and quality standards. Leadership capabilities are tested during transformational and transitional journeys.

Spreading Her Wings Again

The love and support she received from her aging uncle helped her overcome the bouts of depression which had wrecked her for about two years. He had seen her grow and mature into a gifted cheerful girl of 18 when she got married. It was heart-breaking to see her as a young widow with a six-year-old son who looked lost and dazed, not comprehending what had happened to him and his mother.

Her mother was a strong woman and encouraged her to get back to her studies and was prepared to look after her grandson. She went back to the university to take a management degree and was determined to top her batch. Her results in each subject were the best and she stood first in the merit list. She had regained her concentration, confidence and focus which reflected in the results that she achieved.

A large multinational selected her in the HR department. She worked in the corporate office and in the factories in southern and western India. She was posted in the sales locations and also provided HR support to marketing and public relations.

After a successful decade and a half of working, she resigned at the level of a senior general manager as her son, who was 24 and married, needed her time and guidance in the business that he had set up. She looked after the home and partnered with her son and daughter-in-law in the family business which grew from strength to strength. Today, they are owners and leaders of one of the most successful and fastest growing export houses in the country.

At a management convention, a group of people mentioned that she stands out as an example for her ability to connect with people and her persistence to achieve goals and targets that are set by her group of companies. What a saga of courage and fulfilled expectations!

Good leaders know the intrinsic and extrinsic levers for motivating people so that they can have a single-minded focus on results. Results beget results... Nothing succeeds like success!

I met the legendary leader and coach of a world-class cricketer. He said, 'I coached him to make him win every single match as a teenager and to increase his appetite for results and success.'

8

Sharing to Sustain

Generativity is the intense need in a human being to continue living in the memory bank of the universe and be embraced by timelessness and eternity.

The awareness of the transience of life is countered by the need for generativity. This simply is the desire to contribute in any sphere or area which will outlive the person and be useful in the future for posterity. Through generativity a person leaves his or her footprints on the sands of time. Generativity also means taking responsibility to nurture and develop the next generation. It could mean passing knowledge, information, craft and skill to younger people and thus building a legacy for the future. The creative partnership between generations also has its roots in the need for generativity.

Leaders have a strong need for generativity. They are inspired by the need to make a lasting contribution. They would like their contribution and work to outlive them and to be of value for the future.

Generativity expresses itself through many channels and dimensions:

1. The desire to work beyond or transcend the given role and contribute at a much larger level is an expression of generativity.
2. To touch the lives of people and bring about lasting transformation is a manner in which generativity is also expressed.
3. Seminal or breakthrough contributions to knowledge and learning is motivated by generativity.
4. Developing the next generation of leaders is also an expression of generativity.
5. The need and competence to generate creativity in partnership with the young.
6. Building on ideas and working on existing and available knowledge.
7. Contributing towards the realisation of a future vision.
8. Passion to build and shape future advantages.
9. Perceiving the meaning of life from its broadest and deepest wisdom and understanding.
10. Understanding time and space in the long view.

11. Discovering different and more meaningful definitions of love, compassion, empathy, role, contribution and work.
12. Appreciating the connections between body, mind, intellect and soul and putting life in a broader framework.

Daring to Dream

An 18-year-old boy fought with his domineering father and left home to pursue his dream of becoming a lawyer. His father ordered him to leave home. The son left home the same evening. He did not have money and could barely survive for few days which made him borrow cash from a friend. An elderly relative heard his story and his dream, and being a successful and a reputed lawyer, extended financial support for his three-year law degree.

The young man completed his graduation in law and topped the state in the final examination. The academic circles in North India buzzed with news about him and erudite professors felt that the country would be proud to have this genius in law in the future. They were absolutely correct in their assessment. At the age of 35, he became a legal luminary and on a daily basis he was engaged in innumerable cases at high courts across India.

His legal practice was at its peak. Planes were chartered for him by clients to take him to the courts where the cases were listed for hearing. He didn't remember how many appearances or legal arguments he was handling in a day. Then the struggle for the independence of India gathered momentum and leaders reached out to the people of India to join the movement.

He gave up his legal practice, shocking the entire legal fraternity in the country and joined the Quit India movement and worked for the independence of the country. He was jailed for three years and while in jail, lost his wife and his 20-year-old daughter. He bore this guilt and pain throughout his life.

India became independent and he became an active member of the team of experts who drafted the constitution of India. His lasting contribution to the country made his family, the legal fraternity and the country proud. Actively participating in the rebuilding of India he, as a cabinet minister, set the highest standards of integrity for the political offices that he worked for. Then he found time to record his legal experiences and learning in highly acclaimed texts, published and appreciated by a large section of serious readers. They are still invaluable reference material for faculty and students of criminal law. He saw the opportunity to contribute to a larger purpose and for future generations.

Some other insights about generativity:

1. It is not necessary that the need to contribute to a larger purpose becomes strong after personal success in a chosen career. However, often it could lead to a major shift in work.
2. The individual does some pioneering work which benefits large numbers of people. This need seems to be ignited more to serve the poor.
3. It also directs effort towards knowledge, education and learning.

In corporate and other organisations, leaders today value their engagement in developing young talent. This has emerged as a highly researched and professional area of coaching and mentoring. Apart from many others, significant leadership-related competencies are also coaching and mentoring. Many leaders desire to coach and mentor their teams and as well as single individuals in the team. There is a marked difference between coaching and mentoring and their requisite processes and competencies. Mentoring is normally the role of experienced and senior members of organisations who have expertise as well as positional power and authority. Their position and authority in the organisation helps them to take and implement decisions regarding talent management and development. Mentors normally function at the senior and top management levels, keep an eye on the talent pipeline of the organisation and facilitate decisions related to expenditure and resource allocation for their development, learning and training. Their positional power, authority and reputation facilitate decision-making for this task.

Coaching is a process which is directly connected with learning, the facilitation of learning and training and acquiring knowledge and understanding. The coach partners closely with the person being coached and usually partners on a day-to-day basis, more in the initial phase of coaching. Through close interactions, demonstrations and conversations the person observes the coach, obtains suggestions and opinions and picks up the skill or the competency. The coach is process-focussed and supports the person or the team being coached to independently learn while refraining from spoon-feeding. Reviews, close monitoring and feedback suggestions are an important part of coaching. More and more seniors are found coaching their juniors in organisations today and they take pride in their capability to groom young talent. Needless to say that this has always been an area of focus in the Indian Armed Forces (IAF) and officers who demonstrate this capability are awarded coveted positions of instructors in respected institutions like the Wellington Staff College or the College of Combat of the Indian Armed Forces. Senior armed forces officers say with a lot of pride that they groomed so and so Admiral or Brigadier or an Air Marshal. Generativity is indeed a powerful motive in human beings.

The Weak Are Also Strong

The temple has become famous and whoever visits it says that there is a sacred energy and power residing there. Thousands of devotees from all over India walk through the temple corridors and pray to the deity every day. The rich continue to donate large sums of money and the poor give their time and energy towards its upkeep and maintenance. The temple was built by a poor vegetable vendor and its construction cost was nearly three crores about 40 years ago. How did the vendor afford to build the temple? He was poor and had no money to give towards the temple, which is on a three-acre plot, with a built up area of about 10,000 square feet. The best quality material was used for the temple's construction and even after 40 years it is excellently maintained. How did this happen? Where did the money come from? The vegetable vendor was born in a small village across the river Ganga. His parents were small and pious farmers. Unfortunately, they could not afford to educate their six sons and three daughters—they had not inherited any wealth and only eked out a meagre living from their farm. Two sons migrated to the neighbouring city and worked as daily-wage labourers. The daughters married their village friends on their own, sparing their parents the expenditure towards their marriage. The vegetable vendor liked working on the farm and loved growing and selling vegetables.

One day, while cycling down a narrow road connecting his village to a cluster of hamlets nearby, he came across a group of people carrying an unconscious child. They wailed and wept as they walked briskly towards a temple a few kilometres down the road. He came to know that the child was seriously unwell and the doctors had told the parents to take him home. The disease was a terminal one and the child would succumb to the illness within a week. However, some members of the family were convinced that if the child was taken to the temple he would be cured and would live for a long time. The deity was Hanuman who was also known as *sankat mochan*—the god who protects and removes difficulties.

A week later, the vegetable vendor was told by a friend that the child had started recovering. A month later, the news spread in a number of villages that the child was completely well and had started attending school. The doctors felt that this was a miracle.

The vegetable vendor decided to build a Hanuman temple for all the children of the world who would be protected and saved by the deity. His innocence and deep faith inspired him to collect money to build the temple. He cycled for miles and miles for 10 years. He met the rich and the poor, businessman and professionals, men and women, students and teachers, doctors, lawyers, young and old and managed to get large and small donations. He kept selling vegetables to meet the expenditure of his family and gave away all the money which he collected for the construction of the temple. Whenever he saw a child in the temple, his heart was filled with joy and gratitude. Looking at his slim and delicate frame no one could believe that he had the stamina to cycle for almost over 100 miles every day.

I came to know that he passed away two years ago at the ripe age of 95. In the last few years, he had started living in the temple. His body was kept in front of the deity and hundreds of children sang devotional songs and prayed for his soul to rest in peace. Some people give back hugely to life.

Business Asceticism

I don't want to say too much about him because pages and pages have been written about him already. I had three opportunities to see him and witness how he interacted with hundreds and millions of people. He renounced the world in his teens and dedicated his life to spiritual pursuits. His name and fame spread far and wide and donations and gifts flowed to his spiritual centres in abundance. Different people held different opinions about him. However, political, professional and social leaders sat at his feet to receive his blessings. He performed miracles and dazzled the crowds that thronged to these centres.

He has left behind a huge legacy for this country, especially for the poor and the middle class. His schools in almost all the states of India are known for their quality education and academic rigor and a value-based education process. The heart hospital which he constructed is a state-of-the-art facility and treats the poor free of cost. He converted the district in which he was born into a haven of the best civic facilities that people need. The district has excellent educational, medical and administrative support with vocational training for the villagers. This facilitates them to earn a decent living.

The need for generativity propels leaders to do something large and purposeful so that they can leave their mark on the world. It results in taking responsibility to groom future generations through coaching and mentoring and taking pride in being engaged in meaningful contribution. This responsibility could also be towards children in the family and serving the poor and the destitute in society. People who are not able to do this because of lack of opportunity, ill health or their own personality also suffer from feelings of stagnation and mid-life crisis which makes them question the relevance and the rightness of their crucial professional decisions and choices and in later life thereby feel inadequate and regretful. There are a number of people who begin to question the value of their worldly achievements of power, position and wealth as they grow in years. The need to do things close to their heart and also contribute to the larger good catches up. The underlying psychological need for extension or extending ones efforts to touch the lives of others is the foundation of this behaviour. This combined with generativity have made many in their sixties and beyond plunge into large scale social work, even establishing social enterprises and consulting and advisory services for nurturing and developing talent.

9

The Quiet Strength of Acceptance

Acceptance is a source from where mankind draws its contentment and gratitude to remain secure and sane in faith and trust.

By acceptance, I don't mean complacency and a sense of resignation which is borne out of frustration or inertia. Neither is it an attitude to let things be as they are without any effort to improve. Nor is it a tendency to escape from confronting a problem. It is also not avoiding risk and taking up challenges.

Acceptance related to leadership could be explained as:

1. Nature works according to some fundamental principles which, if tampered with, will have adverse outcomes. For example, with advancing age, bodily reflexes will slow down and we must accept this.
2. Some business processes will take time to evolve. Building the company or a product

brand is a long-term process and requires investment.

3. There is always a cost to quality.
4. Everything at all times cannot be controlled. The most powerful chairmen of companies have to lead their businesses according to government policies.
5. Despite high ambition and aspiration, it is good to also be contented with what one has because it sustains gratitude.
6. Accepting that many people could be more talented than us checks arrogance and fosters humility.
7. Accepting the mystery of life, death and destiny increases tolerance.
8. With acceptance, leaders operate from the vantage point of strength and gratitude.
9. Complexity can only be managed by simplicity and clarity and the acceptance of reality.
10. Uncertainty can only be managed by certainty and acceptance gives courage to face facts and the truth.
11. Leaders have to operate in all the three contexts continuously and simultaneously: the context of control, influence and acceptance.

Certain areas of life and work they control, a large area of life and work is always open to be influenced by them, and some aspects of work and life must be accepted as they are.

12. Leaders must also accept that they don't know everything and must learn to face the dynamic and constant change in the business and the social environment.
13. Leaders work with understanding and accept the power of experience, knowledge, information, wisdom and intuition. All these together facilitate the process of steering the progress of individuals and organisations.
14. Leaders accept the power of the team and accept that large and sustainable achievement is only possible through teams. Alone, they can't do very much.

Accepting the Obvious

Here is another interesting story about acceptance and conviction. He was the director of sales and marketing at a huge pharmaceutical company which had operations in India and South East Asia. He had joined the organisation as a management trainee in sales and by the dint of his hard work and the flair to develop relationships with all types of people, he rose rapidly in the sales function. At the age of 38, he became the director of marketing and came to be known in the trade circles as a leader who could win the trust and respect of his team. He was also admired for his deep understanding of the business, the market and the rural context of India.

Girls were aspiring for managerial roles and preparing themselves, through management education, to secure entry into business enterprises. He was not averse to the idea of girls working in managerial positions. In fact in his company, a number of women had excelled in HR, legal and taxation roles since he had joined the company.

However, lately he had noticed a trend in girls to aspire for sales and marketing careers too. He believed that in certain businesses this was possible, such as in hospitality or consumer durables. But certainly not in businesses which operated in remote locations—their products had to be sold in large quantities in practically inaccessible rural interiors of India. Year after year the numbers of girls applying for sales were increasing. There was a pressure on the company from the student community to select girls for the sales function.

He believed that the remote areas of the rural market were unsafe for women to travel alone and stay in small unknown hotels. Hence he insisted that the company would stand by its policy for not inducting women in the sales function. In a large gathering at the open house session in the corporate office, he communicated his conviction on this issue and said that some realities had to be accepted. The physical and psychological safety of women would always be a priority for the company and under no circumstances would the company succumb to pressure from any quarter.

There is a difference between the concept of acceptance and a sense of resignation. There is a certain unfolding of life over which we don't have control. When we sit in the open under the sky and watch the clouds glide past, we don't have any control over the speed and the shapes of the clouds. We could wish that they took a particular shape but that doesn't happen. Our reactive responses could be great disappointment, anger or shedding tears. However, we have to realise that our reactivity will not make the clouds take a different shape. This is just not in our control. That which is not in our control, we must accept. We must accept its happening the way it will happen. Our acceptance is about the shapes and sizes of the cloud. The sense of resignation will mean that we don't give any response. We must respond and choose to respond in the way we think is appropriate. We can leave the place and engage with something else. We can enjoy the shapes that the clouds have taken and we might go a step further and start painting those shapes of the clouds and feel joyous and happy. Accepting how things unfold gives us a lot of freedom to respond to the situation in ways which we find appropriate. In reacting we are often too focused on complaining about why things didn't happen the way we wanted them to. Resignation leads to inaction and acceptance leads to the freedom to respond in an appropriate manner, wherein we exercise our choice and make our independent decisions. Leaders accept situations over which they don't have any control and then exercise their freedom to respond appropriately.

10

Creating Space for Talent

Leaders develop through evolving a healthy consciousness and awareness of transience and impermanence. They, thus prepare to happily hand over the baton to the next line of upcoming leaders for the journey to continue.

Leaders create space for younger people to perform not by abdicating responsibility but by assuming responsibility for developing their juniors so that they are able to perform in important areas of their work. The development of juniors is possible when leaders keep a keen eye on potential and provide timely inputs. They use the process of coaching, feedback, conversations and delegation to facilitate the growth of the young team members for larger and enriched roles.

All leaders are not seen doing this? Why? This can only happen when a leader accepts his or her strengths and weaknesses and believes that big goals can only be achieved through a competent team. The significance of understanding the potential of the team and providing inputs for development becomes an important priority. This creates value and synergy. Once the creative energy of the team is unleashed, the self-confidence of leaders in the capability of the team to perform is enhanced. Leaders are encouraged to delegate and provide additional responsibility to the team.

A leader who works towards making himself redundant makes efforts to personally and professionally grow himself or herself out of his present role. Senior leaders acquire clarity around their professional and personal vision and prepare themselves for larger professional and managerial contributions. They thereby provide space for the younger people to work and develop.

Redundancy is about handing over the baton and about sharing work and experience with juniors and peers. It is not about giving up. Only a leader who enjoys a continuous and upward personal growth himself can assume this responsibility. It also requires immense emotional security and self-confidence. Leaders who have a positive self-image and a high sense of self-worth don't hold their power and authority in a tight grip and don't over-control. They open themselves up for sharing, giving and receiving. Leaders make themselves dispensable and ensure that when they move on other leaders would manage as effectively, if not better, than they did.

Humility also encourages leaders to coach, delegate and develop the team for enlarged roles. Leaders cannot work towards making themselves redundant if they do not believe in the talent and potential of people. The tendency to be astonished at the untapped talent in the world and the passion to see it manifest is also facilitated by humility.

Humility in leaders:

1. Humility makes them listen keenly and sensitively.
2. Humility helps leaders learn from their juniors and also encourage them when they do better than them.
3. Leaders share credit generously and openly.
4. Leaders are open to new ideas and new ways of working.
5. Leaders show pride and assertiveness and not arrogance and aggression.
6. Leaders move from 'I' to 'we'.
7. Leaders connect easily with people from diverse backgrounds.
8. Leaders cope with difficult times by taking responsibility, learning and working with

others. Humility makes them accept their failures with grace and they refrain from putting the blame on others.

Infectious Ease

After completing his masters in economics, he joined a business house in sales and marketing. A simple and humble man, he enjoyed learning from others and was never afraid to admit his mistakes. Seniors loved to delegate work to him because they knew that they could give him feedback, both positive and negative, in an open way. He was always prepared to listen and learn.

From the beginning he showed the qualities of dependability and reliability and readily accepted larger responsibilities. He could discharge these responsibilities successfully as he had the humility to admit his lack of knowledge or skill in some areas and accept guidance from experts.

He rose rapidly in the sales function and at the age of only 35 became the chairman of a division and a member of the management committee of the company.

There is a famous story about him. The company celebrated the launch of a premium brand. For the function and the dinner after the launch, all the senior and the junior managers were invited. As he entered the banquet hall, he noticed the presence of almost 20 middle and junior managers. When the drinks were being served and the atmosphere was a little relaxed, he walked casually and happily towards this group and initiated a conversation.

People spoke about the company, current affairs, which movie they had enjoyed and so on. Then adeptly and skilfully he approached the younger group, pulled a chair, sat down and asked them to tell him where they think he needed to change and the organisation needed to improve and do better. He received very open feedback. Two suggestions were implemented immediately. There were too many feedback forms for the frontline sales staff to fill up regularly. Filling these forms took so much time that no time was left for meeting the trade and even completing the number of beats and visits to retail outlets. The chairman of the division was, at times, too informal and kind. A number of people had started taking advantage of his goodness and compassion. He had to become more demanding with people in the organisation as far as quality and delivery of work was concerned. Gradually the behaviour of the chairman changed. However, he soon realised this and changed his behaviour again—he had the humility to take feedback from the junior-most team member.

When leaders present themselves for feedback on their performance and leadership competencies, they make themselves vulnerable and real. They also subtly shift the processes of review, monitoring and control in the hands of the team. They open themselves to scrutiny and therefore the ownership of the performance of the team is also shifted in the hands of the team. Leaders by doing this, proclaim that they are fallible and not demi-gods and level the ground by reminding the team that although they are leaders their first role is that of a team member. The responsibility of the functioning of the team is not solely theirs but the responsibility of the team too. They are perhaps the first among equals and are therefore prepared to take the larger chunk of the responsibility and accountability. Leaders can't make themselves redundant if they don't create this nature of ownership in the team.

Redundancy is the affirmation of many simple truths:

1. Leadership talent is widely distributed and not the prerogative of only a few.
2. Leaders must realise that young team members must be groomed to take larger

roles because they will grow old both in body and mind. Therefore, contemporary intellectual energy and more physical energy will need to be inducted to keep up with the pace of change and competitive challenge.

3. Developing a strong leadership bench is one of the critical responsibilities of present leaders and unless they gradually include the younger generation in their work this will not be achieved.
4. However, leaders can only be inclusive in their approach once they realise that their contribution lies in coaching, mentoring and in other areas of creative service and stewardship pursuits.

11

Genuinely Great

If you want to see positive, confident and committed men and women, do not keep them happy by pretending to be the person you are not. In the long run, they will respect you for being who you are. You only have to be transparent and genuine.

Genuineness is about walking the talk. This is also about not having a façade or a cover-up. Leaders are seen to be genuine when they do what they say and not have any false pretensions. The perception of genuineness of leaders reduces when they break promises or don't uphold commitments.

Genuineness is important to build business, social and even family relationships. It creates openness and transparency in a relationship. Genuineness is perceived to be an integral part of character building. It is reflected through the congruence of thought, word and action. If there is a gap between what a person believes, says and does people are quick to perceive the gap and lose faith and trust in the person. Once the seeds of doubts are sown, it is difficult to accept the leadership of such an individual. Apart from congruence it is also necessary to show consistency in behaviour so that the reliability and dependability of the person is not doubted. Leaders must be reliable and dependable in order to establish their trust and credibility among their followers. Despite having positional power, once a leader loses credibility and trust, he or she loses respect.

A Touch of Certainty

She is 50 years old. Her children are married and her husband retired from the bank two years ago. She runs a day-and-evening school on the pavement for street children. The school has been functioning for the last eight years in the same place and occupies about 300 square metres of the pavement. When she started the school, she was questioned by the municipal authorities for illegally occupying the space. The police and the citizens living on the road disapproved of the activity and harassed her to leave.

Undaunted she continued and taught the children with dedication and untiring determination. More and more children sought admission and having begun with a batch of nine students, the school now runs four shifts and has a total strength of 206 students. When classes commenced, she was teaching all the subjects herself. However, today she has 17 men and women who have volunteered to teach, and in this way, all the subjects are well covered. The school runs on donation from the rich and the poor. People from all walks of life visit the school and interact with the children. There is enough given in cash and kind to organize books and teaching material, uniforms, *durrees* for the children to sit on and provisions for snacks in the morning and the evening shifts.

She stays in a modest two-room apartment about two kilometres from the school. Her husband has lots of time on his hands and therefore manages household chores and enjoys shopping for the school. He revels in his arithmetic classes and story-telling sessions for junior classes in the school.

Initially the community and authorities thought that this was a money-making racket which she initiated very cleverly under the garb of social service. Many people believed that she had started earning well from the school and her husband, being a banker, was cleverly using his contacts to invest the money. This made a number of neighbours curious and they kept visiting her home to see whether there was an improvement in her lifestyle.

The couple was intelligent and sensitive enough to pick up on these feelings. Without getting too disturbed they continued to work with enthusiasm and left no stone unturned to provide all the advantages possible to the neglected street children. People noticed the growth of the school and the change in the students. The story of the school began to make rounds in political circles and the media got to hear about it too.

The genuine and dedicated leadership of the couple couldn't go unrecognised. Their efforts towards the expansion of the school and improving the quality of the academic processes were appreciated by the students as well as their parents. These families could never have the money to educate their children in this manner. How fortunate were the children to come across the couple who led this movement! Not only did the couple touch the lives of very many children, bringing some hope and certainty to their future, but they also set an example for those who had so much money that they don't know what to do with it. The couple always remained media shy.

Genuineness is also an expression of unconditional love. Despite difficulties genuine people don't change and keep providing love and support. The best example is a mother. No one doubts a mother when she tells her child that she loves her. A mother's love is unconditional and she is giving and caring in all situations. She is with her children through thick and thin and the children have implicit trust and faith in her. A mother may be uneducated but her words of wisdom are respected and she leads her children in her own capacity throughout life. A child very often turns to his mother for advice and she is also a confidante and a trusted friend. Her presence in the world reassures the child that she will always be there to share his happiness and grief. A mother's genuineness is largely not doubted. Often she leads without even knowing that she, in fact, occupies an important leadership role in the family.

Person Perception

It is said that people quickly see through those who pretend to be what they are not. A qualified psychology professor always managed to impress audiences whenever he lectured in sessions inside and outside India. Gradually, he acquired a large fan following not only in the academic circles but also amongst HR professionals working in companies. His name and fame spread far and wide and one day he was appointed the head of the people management function of a large consortium of companies.

He joined the new group of companies with much fanfare. He travelled to company offices and locations, met managers and staff from across functions and businesses in the company. People found him to be poised, articulate and intelligent. Some sensed that he was shrewd and not simple.

He managed the top bosses well and in no time his team was working on extremely sensitive and important HR assignments. One such assignment was of succession planning. For this assignment, he had to closely work with the members of the management committee of the companies in the group as well as with some members of the company board. He heard that the position of the director of HR could be elevated to the company board in the near future.

His working hours in the office became longer and he would be in office till late in the evening. The evening hours were spent in waiting for the board members for five minutes of chit-chat. His team members began to find this a little odd and soon the office began gossiping about this. Some quite unusual things started happening in senior-level meetings. The team members openly complained and began to bitterly blame, shout and scream at each other.

They also distorted data and facts. The HR director would intervene to pacify conflicts and play the wise facilitator in these meetings. This went on for several months till one day one director blurted out in a heated meeting that the HR director had told him how disrespectfully the finance director talked about him to the young managers in the corporate office. He poured out all the data and the false accusations that were bothering him for weeks.

The director of finance was shocked at these allegations and conveyed to the team that there was not even an iota of truth in these allegations. In an investigation, it was revealed that the desire to be on the board made the HR director initiate this politics amongst the directors. In doing so, he believed that a few directors would be in favour of his being elevated to the board.

The organisation managed this discretely and gracefully and then took the decision to ask him to resign from the services of the company. The top leadership felt that the seniors have to set examples of truthfulness, fairness and genuineness and also walk the talk. His behaviour was very different from the espoused values of the consortium.

Genuineness, therefore, is a gateway for establishing trust, credibility and respect. Relationships and communication are strengthened with transparency and authenticity leading to an atmosphere of ease and comfort. In such an atmosphere at the work place or in the family, people have reason to celebrate who they are, their special gifts and interests. The most important thing is the reduction of fear and facade.

12

The Astute Eye

Astute leaders know that in the final analysis, it is a matter of survival in a world which is cold and merciless. It also connotes cunning and shrewdness. The elementary rules are vigilance and agility.

The word 'astuteness' evokes negative connotations like cunningness, cleverness and manipulation. However, for leaders, astuteness or shrewdness could also be a positive quality. In a complex and changing world, leaders have to understand the motives of people and their unstated agendas. There are people who are not straight, those who are selfish and destructive. There is damaging politics in organisations. There is dangerous power play all over the world, not only resulting in the destruction of resources but also of innocent lives and nature. Therefore, a shrewd leader brings in a sharp and quick understanding of this complexity in the team and in the organisation which he leads.

Shrewdness here would be prudence, high sensitivity, tact, judiciousness and emotional maturity.

It would also mean not being naïve but worldly wise and perhaps demonstrating a strategic sense. In other words, it denotes not being vulnerable and not allowing anyone to take you for a ride. Astuteness would also indicate the ability to consider all the variables in the planning and execution process, the obvious and not-so-obvious. It is taking the short and the long-term in view and identifying the positive and negative pressures, their sources, how they operate and how they can be handled.

Leaders who are shrewd appear to weigh the pros and cons of a decision carefully. They know how to play their cards well, have a great sense of timing and the required elan. Even though they might enjoy the romance of achievements, they foresee the possibility of pain and struggle in the process as also the conflicts which have to be tackled or required to be assuaged ruthlessly.

Beyond the Convent Walls

She was a nun in a convent and was known for her leadership capabilities. Teaching geography to the senior classes, she was also in charge of all the events that were annually held at the school. These events demanded a high level of networking and organising. Events such as the annual sports, the cultural festival and the fete also needed financial support, not only from the school but from other institutions in the city. Some well-known and well-to-do citizens of the city always sponsored such activities.

Her school, year after year, bagged the large sponsorships. People talked about this. Many wanted to know why and how she managed to obtain funds for her school. Why? She wanted the school to stand out as the best and bag all the awards and accolades. How? There were only a few ways in which she could lead the school and the students to various victories—they were making the girls work very hard in academics as well as in the co-curricular activities. They were putting in hours and hours of work after school. She could also convince the principal to organise extra rounds of the school bus for those girls who stayed far and who were held up late because of practice sessions. The school didn't charge the girls for these extra bus trips.

Parents of students knew her, parents of children who were studying in other schools had heard about her. The city administration knew about her capabilities. The commissioner of the city, the deputy collectors and the state education department had interacted with her on many occasions and were duly impressed. She intelligently helped people in admissions, granting leave in a difficult situation or employing a teacher who was known to these bodies. Someone asked her about her views on leadership to which she had responded 'What do you mean leading the school? It cannot be lead if I forget what is happening outside it.'

The Wise Are Worldly-Wise

She was brought up in a traditional South Indian Brahmin family. Throughout her childhood she had seen astrologers coming home and reading horoscopes of all the family members. About herself, she had heard that apparently her life would be full of struggle. However, she would never succumb to these pressures and manage her problems and difficulties with astuteness. Comprehending the meaning of astuteness was not easy. As she grew and reached higher classes, her English vocabulary increased and she could understand the word better. Then her grandmother would narrate stories of people who were astute.

The dictionary meaning and the explanations of her grandmother explained the meaning of astuteness.

Grandmother believed that astute people didn't get carried away by praise and flattery and were good at understanding the inner motives of others. Their experience told them that things were not as simple as they appeared to be and therefore they should be measured in their communication so that others would not be able to misinterpret or misuse what they said. Moreover she was convinced that people did not generally like others to be happy or succeed.

The pundits had said that as the planet Jupiter was in the ascendant in her horoscope, she would always be astute, wise and shrewd. She did well in academics and later achieved a lot professionally. She was married off into a rich family of doctors belonging to the same community. Her husband was the youngest amongst his four brothers. All the brothers were doctors and her father-in-law had also made a name for himself in neurosurgery, working in a famous government hospital in the city. He was aging and was not keeping too well and the family insisted that he reduce the number of hours he spent at work.

Her husband's two brothers were employed as senior doctors in a private hospital and were doing well. Her husband and the other brother were running their own clinics. The family was monetarily and materially very comfortable and professionally, they were highly respected. Her mother-in-law was a quiet, humble and a pious woman, bullied by her husband and her sons. The other daughters-in-law cleverly extracted work and money from her and never had a kind word to say to her. She had developed respect and affection for her mother-in-law from the moment she had stepped into the house.

She delivered a beautiful son who made the family joyful on his arrival. Girls outnumbered boys in the family and as soon as he was born it was decided that after completing his medicine he would happily shoulder the responsibility of his father's clinic—so much for individual free will and choice. Nothing went unnoticed by her and as a mother she prayed silently for her son. She was certain that he would find opportunities and a vocation which would make him personally happy. She knew that if she was still alive when these choices were being made, she would encourage him to decide his own path.

There were undercurrents of resentment and politics in the family. Joint families provide physical and to some extent emotional security. However, the system poses tremendous challenges in managing complex relationships. The various shades and hues of positive and negative emotions burden the familial system from time to time. Some emotions are expressed openly, but most times they are suppressed and keep surfacing in other, often physiological, ways—like through a fever or a cold, a backache, mood swings, insomnia or just going out of the house for long hours every evening. The youngest daughter-in-law noticed that her husband's absence from the house was increasing and he would find any pretext to be away from home in the evening, missing dinner with the family. It worried her and she became irritable and seemed to be on the edge most of the times. The three other women other than her mother-in-law, were not being helpful and derived malicious pleasure whenever their mother-in-law was belittled for making an innocent observation about the naughty pranks of the children that led to complaints by the neighbours.

One night she lay awake and thought that if the situation at home continued to drift like it was, it would become even more nasty and unbearable. Very soon one of the brothers would decide to move out. With the first exodus, the trend to escape would begin to deepen the scars and the cracks and eventually the family ties would snap. The family would also lose its professional standing and strength.

As the population grew in the city, clinics and nursing homes mushroomed rapidly. She was certain that the big fish would swallow them as they were still small compared to the rest of the medical world and would not be able to compete with organised businesses like big hospitals and state-of-the-art nursing homes. Gradually the future course of decisions and actions became clear, making her confident about speaking with the entire family. Two aspects were important—keeping the family together as a unit through sustained respect, love and trust in family relationships and bringing back transparency in communication. This had to be handled well, not only for the brothers and their spouses but more for the well-being of the children—for their emotional and psychological security. The other important aspect was the financial strength of the family. If the brothers stayed and worked together their work and wealth would also keep growing.

She invited her sisters-in-law for coffee at a Barista outlet which was close to the house. The reason given by her was that she was overjoyed to receive the news of her brother becoming a father and wanted to celebrate with her peers. All the women of the house appreciated this gesture and they happily accompanied her for coffee that morning. In retrospect, it is evident that fate and destiny were impatiently waiting for the door to open so they could enter. The goddess of destiny entered her family and changed everything.

The sisters-in-law were impressed with her intelligence and intent and agreed that the family should stay together at any cost. The brothers and the parents accepted the logic and the well-being of the children became the most important consideration. The brothers decided to set up a hospital with money raised from banks and other sources. While they decided to burn the midnight oil, their wives and parents took charge of the home, day-to-day chores and social obligations. The larger goal and purpose brought in trust and love, which the family had not experienced earlier or in its entire history. There was joy and excitement of achievement. Little compromises that were made from time to time were worth the happiness and wellness that became theirs. Today her family is a force to be reckoned with. The hospital has seen unprecedented growth with five branches in the city. A few boys from the next generation are ambitious doctors and entrepreneurs, having established a pharmaceutical manufacturing facility and company. The daughters are well married. The father-in-law passed away a happy and contented man and blessed her. Her mother-in-law is respected and loved by the grandchildren.

That coffee meeting was the turning point. Her wisdom, astuteness and shrewd timing became a master stroke in the face of rising professional competition between the men of the family. It also made the women converge at the right time and over right decisions. She influenced them by keeping the mirror in front and clarified the emerging big picture of success and the demands and the outcomes of family support. Her son became a reputed architect and loved his mother for encouraging and understanding him. He told his friends one day, 'She is the wise and clever one in the family.'

Shrewdness and astuteness in a familial setting means:

1. Understanding complex aspirations and ambitions.
2. Competitiveness also exists in families and can become very destructive if not handled wisely.
3. Anything substantial for families to achieve is only possible when family members stay together in solidarity and some family members facilitate the bonding process.
4. Positive influence has to be exerted on the family from time to time.

5. Families are also impacted by negative power dynamics. This emanates from hierarchical positions and gender inequality. Normally male members have more influence over important family decisions. However, of late, it is seen that the position of women in families is becoming more influential.
6. Wisdom lies in keeping the personal vision of the family members aligned with the family vision and keeping a tight hold and keen focus on family values. The cultural norms of the family cannot be diluted under any circumstances.
7. An eye is to be kept on the opportunities by the family for advancement in wealth and prosperity. No family can remain happy and together for long if family members do not work towards augmenting the wealth and status of the family. There is a lot of merit in staying and working together.

Astuteness and shrewdness are often political. A shrewd and astute person understands the apparent as well as the subtle political dynamics in a situation. Politics is largely concerned with power, control and influence. Astuteness does not neglect power dynamics, the ability to influence decision-making and being close to people who can make things happen. Leadership is not just about motivation, inspiration and empathy. It is also about having a keen strategic sense and the ability to scan the environment for opportunities. Astute individuals strike partnerships and alliances with those who can assist them in obtaining opportunities and resources to implement their plans. They can nurture support systems for themselves so that these networks give them strength. However, true strategic capability creates a win-win for partners and such wins are fairly negotiated keeping in mind long term benefits for both.

From the leadership perspective, astuteness must be considered as a dimension of wisdom and not an element of craftiness and cunning. In this book, leadership is only explored from the perspective and frameworks of positivity and constructive contribution. There are leaders and have been leaders, who have created negative results and mass destruction for people and civilisations. We are not covering those destructive leadership behaviours, processes and forces. Therefore even shrewdness is being defined in the larger perspective of wisdom which obtains a win-win for both parties included.

It is seemingly difficult to survive without astuteness because it does bring practicality to decisions and thinking, highlights the need to be careful and consider both the positive and the negative outcomes.

13

Expedient Expertise

Expedience is opportunistic and transactional. The give and take is short-lived and the gains are also not evenly distributed. However, the law of the jungle is hard reality. There is a struggle for winning and losing and we tell ourselves that 'all is fair in war and victory'. However, from the positive leadership behavioural framework, even expediency in the long-term is squared off.

To be expedient is to make a conscious decision to use a situation, an opportunity or a person for personal, professional, organisational or national advantage. The decision is for the short-term, for quick gains and the relationships are short-lived and snap once the transactions are over. In an expedient approach, the individual who initiates action knows what he wishes to gain and decides to use the situation or the other person. In any case the others, after a while, feel used and victimised. However, even though the relationships are short-lived, the leaders know that if the relationships are valued the gains have to be for both parties and they must contribute towards their achievement as well.

Many leaders are known to display this behaviour from time to time. Some say that this demonstrates their pragmatism and astuteness. It is believed that this helps in staying ahead of the competition and being better equipped for survival when resources are less and there are pressures for the achievement of stretched targets.

Expediency, therefore, is a set of behaviours of leaders that demonstrate:

1. Awareness that resources are limited and that one has to be constantly alert and vigilant and use the opportunities and people to one's own advantage.
2. Tactical capability wherein advantages are garnered for the team and the self at the cost of others, in the short-term.
3. An assumption that if we don't do this, then the others will definitely take advantage of us and the situation.
4. A belief that this is a part of a mature and shrewd understanding of the market place and the world in general and helps in being completely realistic.

5. The dictum of 'survival of the fittest'.
6. Intelligence, cleverness, protective and supportive behaviour of the leader.
7. It is not selfish.
8. It is a part of the complex political nature of human beings and the socio-political reality which thus gets created.
9. It mitigates the long-term survival of relationships and achievements. The foundations built are extremely flimsy and the relationships lack trust, respect and genuineness.
10. Leaders who largely operate with expediency might win huge short-term successes. But they rarely see sustained excellent performance and achievement. They fail to build lasting processes, character and reputation of the organisations and people whom they lead.

Short and Long Is Not the Same

He came from a middle-class family of one of the southern states in India. His parents were law abiding and hard-working people and wanted all their children to be well-educated and succeed in life. He showed a lot of promise even as a child and the family was convinced that he would achieve a lot in his life. His educational career was above average. When he was 21, he completed his graduation in law. His interest in current affairs and his general knowledge was very impressive. He had an uncanny knack for establishing contacts and relationships with people from all walks of life. Being a lawyer himself, he had contacts with the senior-most lawyers in the country. He personally knew a number of judges and their families as well as the central and state government officials of most of the states and ministries. University students and faculty members were his friends who liberally invited him to academic events, sometimes as a part of the elite audience and sometimes as a lead speaker. His name was becoming widely known and he was also being featured in interviews on various media channels on the television, important professional journals and widely circulated magazines and newspapers. He knew that people knew him and that his name and popularity were increasing. He enjoyed being praised and admired.

As a junior lawyer working in the chamber of a brilliant senior counsel in criminal law, he learnt a lot in nine years. He then decided to leave the senior lawyer's chamber to be on his own. Initially it was not easy to be on his own; it meant taking a sizeable hit on his monthly take-home and other financial earnings by setting up his own office. He was determined to achieve great heights and the love, understanding and support of his wife helped him in the transition. He found a good place for the office near the high court and the railway station. Two bright young lawyers, both nephews of a friend and a successful businessman, agreed to join him. They had a small puja on Diwali in the office and launched work with positivity and joy.

He worked hard with the two young men, and in no time their practice picked up—they made quite a name for themselves. They had to shift to a larger space because the office became crowded in the evenings with clients and their relatives. The new office was twice as large and on moving there, he decided to throw a large dinner for his friends and acquaintances, lawyers, judges, business people and politicians. The young colleagues were uncomfortable with this because they felt that inviting senior judges with politicians and businessmen was not the right thing to do, being against legal protocol and norms. Their suggestion was not accepted and the dinner happened as it was planned. Funnily enough after the dinner, more work flowed in and the earnings, month after month, also increased. Nothing to complain about at all, thought the young lawyers in office.

With an increased workload, it became imperative to recruit in new members in the office on a full-time basis. These were young and senior lawyers. He had a large team and was confident that the team would be able to deliver work very well. Their case-winning rate was very good. They were gaining a reputation for excellent drafting and skilful arguments. A number of high court judges liked him and his team. He worked late into the night in the office with the team and on the weekends and then took off to play golf at the club, read in the club library and also attended music recitals. He was passionate about North Indian classical music.

His personal wealth had increased substantially and now he was in a position to buy a plot of land in one of the upmarket residential areas of the city and build a bungalow. His wife encouraged him and within a year all the decisions were taken. A well-known architect and builder took over the contract and their dream house cost a whopping 64 crores. And then of course, there was a gala where important and influential people of the city made an appearance. Some were also flown in from outside.

The office team did not seem cheerful during the dinner. Some younger members were not even invited. Those who were invited sat together in a corner of the lawn. Their boss was busy looking after the glitterati and didn't find time to interact with them at all. They felt a little humiliated. The two youngsters who were the first to join his office were not invited to the dinner. After a week, he asked them to set up their own practices as they had gained enough experience in his office and as the numbers in the office had become large, it was becoming unmanageable.

This hit them like a bolt from the blue. They felt devastated and knew that it would take them a while to set up a practice on their own. They also didn't have enough money which would sustain them for a year or two. One of them had got married and had a wife and a mother to look after.

They had been with him for now six years and built the office brick by brick. The two youngsters felt very badly let down. Their families were of the opinion that now that he had senior lawyers who got him more money through cases, he didn't want them anymore. They felt that he had used them and treated them callously and unfairly. They began to notice his tendency to manipulate and exploit people.

The farewell of the youngsters was quite a lacklustre event. Some of the junior and senior colleagues were very unhappy at the way they were treated. They could foresee a trend being set for the future. As the years rolled on, the same treatment was meted out to many in the office. Now it was a legal firm with a name and very large accounts. However, it gained a terrible reputation for the way employees were treated. His children did not choose the legal profession. One son became a surgeon and decided to settle in the USA. The daughter did architecture, married an architect and made Bangalore her base.

He was aging and ailing. Unfortunately he did not have anyone dependable and as competent as him to take the firm over. One evening while sipping tea in his beautiful garden, he remembered the two youngsters who had started the office with him. They had the spark, he thought, and could have easily taken the firm to great heights even when he was gone. He was right. They had the spark. They took the firm to great heights. However, the firm was not his but it was their own firm which they established when he had asked them to leave.

Expedient behaviour can be harmless and can lead to a win-win in the long-term. Great leaders are open in partnerships, which they forge and use for short-term personal gain and are ready to be fair in the long-term with partners in sharing gain and creating advantageous opportunities for them. The give and take in the truly expedient transaction which leads to a win-win evens out towards the end. Both the partners work on the principles of fairness. Expedient partnerships are not blindly and completely self-focused or self-centred. On many occasions the strategic thinking of leaders creates expedient partnerships. However, the real successful businessperson, while focusing on short-term gains, would not compromise on the long-term advantages of shared success.

Exploitation is different from expediency, as an exploitative partnership exists only for a short while. The nature of such a partnership is win-lose. If the partnership lasts longer, which in many cases it does, then the partnership ascends to a win-win. The win-lose and win-win spirals continue and for both the parties, the gains keep getting squared off. In exploitative relationships the gain is only of one party. The other party only loses and is the sufferer. Such a relationship continues mainly under pressure and when it snaps, it does so for good.

Many leaders take an exploitative stance while leading organisations and nations. History is full of such examples. It is also common to see that exploitative regimes do not last for long and are followed by rebellions and revolutions. These leaders work by the dint of their power and control over resources, communication, and people. They encourage the formation of coteries and sycophants who become responsible for their later troubles and downfall. Such leaders do not build people, processes or organisations. They build themselves and their families. Exploitation is closely linked with a major lack of personal integrity which is expressed through financial, intellectual and moral dishonesty. Many great organisations and nation states have been destroyed by exploitative leaders.

14

A Bouquet of Versatility

It is a mistake to believe that varied interests and different and contradictory capabilities are rarely present in human beings. There are people with talent in many areas. At times, one is amazed to witness talent for both business and music coexisting in the same person. People wonder how a woman is a world-class playback singer in films and also an entrepreneur who runs a thriving diamond business. Human beings never stop surprising us.

To be versatile is to express talent in multi-dimensional forms. A versatile person is able to do and excel in many areas. A woman can be good in her profession as well as in keeping a beautiful and efficient home. At the same time she could be a good mother and wife and manage the social relationships of the family extremely well.

A corporate leader can be excellent in marketing and in people management at the same time. A factory foreman by the dint of his innate talent and versatility can rise up to the management cadre, later specialise in finance and prepare himself for the membership of the board of the company where strategic thinking and an understanding of the complex socio-political environment is expected together with deft management.

There are different dimensions of human talent that appear to coexist because they originate from the same source, for example the quality to nurture good relationships and the capability to counsel and coach. Both revolve around the ability to build relationships. Some people display different and distinct talents like being good at mathematics and also painting. Mathematics deals with numbers, logic and concrete thinking. Therefore, how can the same individual be good in painting and mathematics if painting requires emotional sensitivity and imagination, abstraction and design capability? Talent is abundant and present in many forms. Multi-dimensionality of talent makes an individual versatile which makes him multitask and become multi-skilled.

Combination and Completeness

He did not have formal academic qualifications. He was just a graduate in English literature. At the age of 20, he joined a British company in Mumbai in the sales function. The company was a FMCG giant, selling food products all over India. He went through a year of rigorous training in sales. Communication was his strength and his fluency in English was admirable. His family atmosphere contributed immensely to his grooming and personality. There was a charm in the manner in which he interacted with people. His varied interests in theatre, music and Urdu poetry impressed the young and the old. His manners and etiquette won the hearts of people in his social circle as well as those in office. What a voice! Whoever heard him converse or speak in public said that he was a rare human being.

Ten years in the company flew by quickly. Learning and absorbing the complexities of business management and marketing, he grew in the function and was soon heading a region in South India. His achievements were not exceptional but were certainly commendable. However, his senior and he himself knew that that the level of incompetence in the function would hit him fast. There were many others in the company who were smarter and doing much better than him.

The time he spent at the theatres in the evenings was increasing and gradually he realised that what he enjoyed doing the most was being with people and developing them. This, it appeared, was also the reason for his love for theatre. One bright sunny morning, as he drove to office, he decided to request his senior for a meeting. Shifting to HR became a strong desire and he looked forward to his senior's guidance. They met over coffee. It was a long, open and a thoughtful discussion. His senior asked some sharp questions and confronted him with negative feedback about his poor grip on the financials in sales and that after a certain seniority level managing the financials effectively is an important requirement of any function. Was he trying to escape from responsibility?

The senior recognised his flair for handling people. Concerned about the lack of a formal education in HR, he felt that the other professionally-qualified peers and seniors would be a force to reckon with. According to him, HR as a professional discipline and a subject was developing and evolving. It was a specialisation and his formal qualification was limited to only a few management development programs and short-term courses. Formal and full-fledged degree programs, with their rigor, give a depth of understanding and clarity of concepts and constructs which shorter teaching modules do not provide.

He felt disturbed about his inadequacy but was determined to work hard and knew that he would speed up and develop deep theoretical knowledge in the area as he was a voracious and enthusiastic reader and learner. He was transferred to the corporate HR function.

He joined various courses and HR forums. His voice and command over English were of great advantage for this work. An intrinsic interest in people helped him to comprehend their issues quickly. The company noticed his progress in the function. Soon he was given the charge to head learning and development in the larger divisions of the organisations. His contribution in leadership development and redesigning a number of HR systems such as the recruitment process, the entire induction programme and the appraisal format and process were appreciated by the senior management.

The professional behavioural forums and programs in India invited him to lecture, chair seminars and lead many HR interventions. Then one day the chairman of the company held a special meeting of the management committee and restructured the HR corporate and the divisional HR function. It was decided to hand over the entire developmental HR aspect to him because of the extremely good work that he had done. He had also developed a strong team in HR in a very short period.

Anthropology, theatre, music and poetry were his other passionate interests. In fact his contribution to theatre, both in acting and in script-writing, was amazing and he groomed a number of youngsters who became famous stage artists and film stars.

This man was truly versatile and led his expanding HR team with his versatility which encouraged his team members to pursue their interests and hobbies and helped them evolve as more complete and rounded human beings.

We live in very interesting times, replete with disruption and diversity which demand versatility of skills and styles for successfully managing and responding to transformational challenges. First and foremost leaders need to display flexibility in thinking and action as each situation and person that they deal with pose dissimilar demands and pressures. Young managers occupying senior positions have to be handled in a certain way, women colleagues have their own needs and ways of behaving, technology disrupts processes sooner than later and new skills are required to be mastered fast. There are a medley of traditions and mindsets in organisations because of the multi-cultural and ethnically diverse workforce. To top it all off, people have reworked the definitions of commitment and motivation in so far as pay cheques are fast losing their capacity to pull in people and are replaced by many other advantages that people seek from organisational careers such as opportunities to learn. So leaders cannot rely on just a few time-tested inputs and skills of leading. Leadership has come to mean innovative capability and versatility in responding to multi-dimensional talent which is manifested in the process. This facilitates leaders to master divergence and disruption and keep on learning and enjoying the journey of personal evolution and growth.

From Potential to Performance

This story is quite unbelievable. He had joined a large multinational as a trainee in the sourcing and purchase function. He spent almost 15 years in these functions and contributed to the growth of the departments substantially while also leading the teams effectively. He was a good negotiator and had a continuous eye on vendor development. He earned a reputation of very high dependability and integrity. The organisation in which he worked was doing well and was in the throes of major expansion and diversification. He reported to the deputy chairman of the company who was known for his uncanny knack for spotting hidden talent. Being extremely likeable and polite, the deputy chairman developed a lot of affection for him and their relationship also became one that was personal, close and strong.

His mother had brought him up, had worked very hard to earn to run the house, pay for his education and later for his marriage and his settling into a fairly decent house. Being the only child, and having lost his father in his teens, he had deep affection and admiration for her and felt very grateful to her for what she had done for him. It was her 70th birthday and he wanted to celebrate it well. He'd been an excellent cook all his life and was passionate about cooking, not just ordinary daily food but fancy cuisine which he kept trying from recipe books on weekends and holidays. On the day of the dinner, most of the food was cooked by him—it was quite a spread and excellently prepared. The guests were all praises for his culinary flair and they said that he was gifted with this unique talent. The deputy chairman also attended the dinner and was greatly impressed with his talent for cooking.

A week later he was suddenly called for a late afternoon meeting to the deputy chairman's office. It was known in the company that whenever the deputy chairman had this type of a meeting, it was always for an unusual issue, which after finishing all his work for the day, he liked discussing till late in the evening. The deputy chairman again congratulated him for the wonderful dinner and food on the occasion of his mother's birthday. Then there were a volley of questions about his interest in cooking, what all he could cook, how often he cooked, what his other interests were and so on. Why hadn't he thought of devoting all his time to something he was so good at? Did he know that the hotel industry all over the world had become very professionally managed? And then the real conversation commenced. Their company was planning to diversify in a major way into the hospitality business and was about to set up a chain of five-star hotels. The deputy chairman suggested that his talent could be utilised and he be formally trained to head the food and beverages side of the business and also become the corporate chef for the chain in India and overseas.

He thought that the deputy chairman perhaps was not well and under a lot of stress, hence he had lost his sense of proportion totally. How could a man who spent 15 years of his career in material sourcing and purchase, and cooked only as a hobby, head the food and beverages—a highly specialised area of the hospitality business—department and evolve into a chef? Was the deputy chairman all right? What was going wrong with the company? He couldn't respond and kept mumbling how grateful he was for the appreciation and encouragement by the chairman and that he would need time to think. He immediately went up to a lady colleague and narrated what had transpired in the meeting. He knew that there was an exercise of restructuring on in the company and he had heard rumours that some functions would be downsized. Gripped by the sudden fear of losing his job, he dreaded to think that his name was also on the list of those who could be asked to leave. The deputy chairman could be indirectly hinting at this.

He came home and shared his apprehension with his wife. He had two young school-going children and did not inherit any wealth from his family. Strange are the ways of life. His fears were completely unfounded. The board of the company had reposed it's faith in the deputy chairman for manning the hospitality business. The deputy chairman was completely convinced about what he was planning to do with the decision to convert a manager of purchase and sourcing into a corporate chef.

He was sent for training overseas to the best culinary college for a year. He trained wonderfully well, returned to establish and head the food and beverages function and also became the corporate chef of the chain. After two years, his name appeared on the list of 300 best chefs in the world. After six months he was also given additional charge to head the purchase function for the chain as the company completely relied on his competence and integrity. What versatile talent and what foresight and courage by the company to utilise it so well!

Mothers are capable of a lot of multi-tasking. They lead by keenly observing and motivating their children and others too. They manage relationships well and can also cook exceptionally well. A number of mothers are excellent in inventory management and even in managing money. Their husbands and children rely on them for they know that it's the first lady of the house who will bail them out. They lead in emotional intelligence and a number of mothers are rock-solid in times of trouble and crisis. They don't seem to lose their cool. I would like to share something about my mother with you.

She Is Still My Strength

At the age of 18, she with her parents and other siblings, fled from Pakistan and came to India during the partition. Traumatised by witnessing the communal violence, and losing all material comfort and security the family had to start life afresh.

She married my father at the age of 21 and bore him three children by the time she was 25. Being innately aesthetic and house proud, she gave us a beautiful and an elegant home. We all looked forward to spending time at home because it was so beautiful and cheerful. I remember a cool October evening when I was back from school on a Saturday with a few friends. My mother was sitting in the veranda chopping vegetables for dinner and looking ethereally beautiful. She impressed my friends with her impeccable spoken English and the food she prepared for us.

A voracious reader and always updated on current affairs, she could hold her own in legal and political gatherings as my family was in law and politics. We felt proud of her intellect and the way she carried herself.

A source of confidence for the family, she had nerves of steel and could weather many storms without getting rattled. I remember the courage with which she faced my father's fatal illness and the dire financial situation in that period. She was like a rock and led from the front. My father believed that she was the engine in the train of our lives and we were the wagons which tugged along behind her power and direction. Her multifaceted personality and innate versatility was a gift for us. I as her daughter learnt the power of silence and emotional strength from her. She was a guide and philosopher and mentored and guided me to come out of my personal tragedy, strong and confident, when I lost my husband. She was a pillar of strength and showed me the way to rebuild my life again. She led the social side of the family and also led the development of her children. She is still my strength because mothers don't pass away, they live through their daughters.

15

Awesome Respect

People are respected when they exemplify the core and cherished values of society. People are also respected for their character and competence. Respect is earned and commanded. In the final analysis people are respected for who they are and not for their position, power or wealth.

Incorruptible Courage

He led the high court as the chief justice for two years. Lawyers and judges in the high court had never witnessed the level of personal integrity which he possessed. He was immensely admired for his legal acumen and brilliance. However, he was held in awe for his complete and undiluted honesty and his purity of thought and feeling. Described as fair to the core, with no malice and bias, he displayed the highest standards of ethics in his decisions and dealings with all concerned in the courts of law. The high court proudly proclaims incredible tales of his unblemished reputation.

One of the states in North India was in political and social turmoil. The region had been torn with conflict and war for decades, without any hope for solutions and settlement. Tugging along, the government did it's best to maintain a superficial calm by finding short-term solutions, sometimes playing religion and caste against each other and at other times resorting to appeasing people by populist decisions such as reducing food prices, giving free education and holding medical camps for the poor in the remote mountainous locations of the state.

The then prime minister of India decided to request him to consider being transferred to the trouble-infested state as the chief justice of the state high court. The prime minister and the government underestimated his integrity and courage and adopted the same modus operandi as they would have done with others assuming that he, like some others, would succumb to the pressures of political power and threat and the temptation of money.

A judge visited him in the evening with the message from the prime minister regarding the transfer offer and also asking him to meet the prime minister in the circuit house. For the man he was, he must have been greatly angered by the audacity of the government officials to approach him directly. He maintained his calm and with great restraint and dignity conveyed to them that being a sitting judge of the high court, it would not be correct for him to meet politicians. It would be appropriate and within judicial norms if the prime minister found time, took an appointment and came to meet him in his chamber at the high court.

His response sent a tremor in government circles. The state and central government officials who were involved in this matter did not know how to respond and what to communicate to the prime minister. He had also conveyed to them that he did not discuss money matters with anyone except those who dealt with his salary and other related accounts in the high court.

Surprisingly the prime minister did not react at all and wisely dropped the issue. It was never discussed again in the government and political circles. He was later told that the decision was to transfer him as he belonged to the northern state and the government believed that this would calm down, to a considerable extent, the frustrations and the disturbance in that state and its judiciary.

The wife of the judge was anxious for weeks and was convinced that her husband would be impeached by the president of India on some false charge soon. She shared her apprehension with her husband. Characteristically he responded, 'Don't worry so much, they can only impeach me, not take my life.'

On his death many said that they had not seen so many cry and breakdown at a funeral procession like they saw when he was being carried for his cremation. The government officials, who had participated in the episode of his transfer decision which could not be implemented, were also there. Years later, they specially flew from the capital to attend the funeral. The officials attending his funeral stood with their heads bowed in respect, awe and admiration for a man who refused to be corrupted and led the administration in the high court with the highest order of personal integrity.

Respect and trust are closely connected and it is difficult to establish which comes first and which comes after. Trust can be defined simply by words like dependability and reliability. What a person says he does and therefore, people believe in him or her. It also means you believe that the person whom you trust can never harm or hurt you in any way. They always wish the best for you and act for your welfare and advantage. Trust is created between people when commitments are upheld. Commitment means keeping promises and not letting someone down. People repose trust in those who lead them and when their trust is kept, respect for leaders is enhanced.

16

Lessons on Leadership

Leaders work towards achieving results today and tomorrow. They also create strong foundations for organisations. They co-create a vision for the emerging, unfolding and limitless future and navigate the journey for converting latent potential into demonstrable performance. Leaders work both towards tangible and intangible results. They are also focused on the purpose and larger goals. Not only do they manage complex changes, but they also manage the growth of organisations, teams and individuals. They manage difficulty and contradictions. Leaders manage rising and complex aspirations and also integrate the good of the past with the challenges of the present. They manage and utilise power. Leaders help generate meaning, which in turn creates high levels of shared purpose and commitment.

Often leaders are deep thinkers—they are perceptive, sensitive, can simplify matters and situations, can integrate, relate and connect, can wait and be patient, can influence and be assertive and can energise, communicate and analyse. They take risks, and initiatives. They listen deeply and actively, lead from the front and get their hands dirty. They control their emotions, tolerate frustration and disappointment and persist. They are usually intuitive, optimistic and positive people who can outsmart the other person. They have high awareness and networks, they are disciplined and focused, prepared, look at things differently, and are ahead of their times. They can multitask, work and live with multiple perspectives and they manage proximity and distance well.

I have seen that all leaders cannot do all these things well. Leaders contribute in four main and distinct areas and this depends on their abilities and interests. Some have the competence to contribute well in one area and not so well in the others. In my understanding the four main areas of leadership contribution are the following.

Vision

Leaders have the capability for envisioning the future, conceptualising and articulating the larger goals and purpose of the organisation. Leaders focused on the future have the courage to intervene and co-create it and exhibit an understanding that others don't. The envisioned future of the organisation is created with the important stakeholders of the organisation. Leaders also have the ability to articulate that vision and communicate it. Visionary leaders work with multiple perspectives and take a long view. They see the whole, the gestalt, the systemic and the integrated reality of organisations and life. They have the ability to connect the apparent contradictions of the past, present and the future. They have the understanding of the inherent strength in legacies inherited from the past, the opportunities and the strengths available in the present and the latent potential available to be built on and manifested tomorrow.

These leaders knit together a framework of work and personal values and also enunciate them within the organisation as well as across the entire stakeholder network. These values are the stepping stones towards the envisioned future. No vision can be realised without the guidance and the directions set by instrumental values which define things that are important and how they should and will be achieved respectively. Inherent in these values are the purpose and the large goals for work, and the way these will be obtained.

A lot of work which leaders in the vision area do facilitates the building of national and organisational cultures. Shared values are the foundation of culture. These values are identified together and obtaining the buy-in of all the stakeholders to these values is critical. Communication across organisations about vision and values is encouraged, people are encouraged to talk about the values that they hold dear and would like their work and organisations to uphold too.

Visionary leaders also motivate all stakeholders around the stated purpose of the organisation. Many people in the organisations may not understand the difference between vision, purpose, goals and targets. I would like to attempt defining and differentiating the meanings:

1. Vision is the dream for the future. It emanates from the possibilities perceived by the leaders and all other stakeholders of the organisation. It is the picture of the organisation as it evolves and is visualised defining its areas of engagement, contribution, its standards of quality and scale, size of operations and possible achievements. An example of the vision would be—'An organisation which will provide excellent people-management services, understanding and solutions in consulting and also publish its cutting edge

knowledge across the globe so that it can share with the professional world the latest information in the people-management sphere'.

2. Purpose defines the reasons why such an organisation must exist and why society and customers should give it the sanction for existence. The purpose behind the vision of the consulting firm would be—'The dissemination of knowledge in diverse organisations across the world. The purpose is in the area of enhanced understanding, communication and application of solutions, innovation and growth'.
3. Goals are the broad areas of aspired contribution. Broad goals for the HR consulting firm could be—'Working in the area of leadership development, both in private and public sector organisations. The focus will be to develop the leadership bench strength at the middle-management level so it may aid in career planning, growth planning and succession planning processes in a more scientific manner'.
4. Targets are related to specific projects in the leadership development area Targets

> for leadership development for a consulting assignment at the middle-management level could be more role-specific, focussed on specific deliverables like the development of technical, managerial and leadership competencies required in middle-management positions. Deliverables will also have timelines, quantitative and qualitative measures and assessment criteria for leadership competencies. These will also be business and context specific. The expected outputs by leaders at the middle-management positions will also be defined and their measurement and assessment criteria detailed.
>
> Leaders appear to be contributing to some areas and even though these are connected with each other, leaders have more talent in some of these areas over others.

Related to the organisation vision and the organisational culture building efforts, leaders who contribute largely in this area also have the capability to inspire stakeholders to understand the vision and to own it. Many visionary leaders have inspired members of organisations and motivated them to commit their efforts for working towards the vision. Therefore energy is deployed for co-creating the future vision and people take major responsibility for achieving it. Visionary leaders are often seen to be competing with themselves and set very high performance standards. They feel deeply and are sensitive and don't lose hope. They can rise above narrow concerns.

However, the negative side of visionary leaders is that they could also live in their own world. They might get disconnected with today's reality and could also be disconnected with a number of people at the junior levels and in the frontline of the organisations. At times they tend to get fearful, anxious and insecure and feel that most people don't understand them.

Transformation

These leaders are adept in understanding and managing change. They are the agents of change in organisations. Every organisation requires leadership talent in the area of managing change, entrepreneurship and managing transition. These leaders facilitate in the translation, communication and the embedding of the vision of the organisation. They are seen to work closely with other visionary leaders. Leaders are good at confronting issues and problems, in giving and receiving open and transparent feedback and are not uncomfortable with uncertainty and ambiguity.

They are good listeners and are expansive and tolerant. They also have the ability to manage complexity. They can be excellent coaches, counsellors and facilitators. They themselves are generative and have a high need for extension. They love institution-building and organisational turnarounds. They can translate the vision into significant thrust areas for future work in the organisation. Since they are knowledgeable themselves, they are seen to bring in high levels of academic rigour and erudition. They are loyal to the visionary leader and tend to stay with him for a number of years. They obtain reflected power and can manage it with humility. They shun the limelight and work in the background. They influence and facilitate the visionary leader to communicate the vision. They might not have formal organisational position, hierarchical authority and designation.

Transformational leaders understand the whole business broadly and also have an uncanny knack to decipher the external and internal environmental opportunities, strengths, weaknesses and threats. The visionary leader trusts them, listens to them and respects them. He or she feels secure with them and is also close to them personally.

Transformational leaders thrive on the given freedom and space, opportunities to innovate and work on organisation-wide processes.

Strategy

Then there are strategic leaders. A strategy is the approach and the competence to gain competitive advantage through both the tactical and long-term plan and its implementation. The strategic leader works on how the vision can be translated into both long-term and short-term goals and plans. Leaders in this area of work also see how best these goals can be executed and implemented. These leaders are thinkers and busy themselves with data, information and trends. They also work at critical-decision areas about what to do and why and when to do it and arrive at conclusions after thoroughly analysing issues, problems and opportunities. They look at gaps to be filled, created by emerging opportunities and threats. The numbers and figures of the businesses of competitors are thoroughly scrutinised by them. They track and analyse their postures and plans and look at winning strategies which may help in achieving the best outcomes and results. They work with a keen sense of time and work to take advantage of the weak areas of competitors.

Strategic leaders put the company in the context of various visualised scenarios of advantages and disadvantages and set definite directions of work to be undertaken. Not only that, they also establish how that work should be approached and executed. They also review roles, responsibilities, structures, systems, processes and procedures required for achieving strategic goals and strategic plans. Criteria and measures and metrics for monitoring and appraisal of performances are also matters for serious deliberation for these leaders. Leaders in this segment prepare the game plan.

Operations

Operational leaders manage the performance of those who actually work and execute strategic and operational plans. This also includes all the frontline workers. The game plan is handed over to the operational leaders. For executing it well, the operational leaders work on methods, systems and processes of the plans. Operational leaders deploy company resources on a day-to-day basis and work towards establishing and reviewing processes and systems. They build capability and develop operational talent. They also get into the nitty-gritty of time planning.

Their role also includes building a culture of high performance and flawless execution. Keeping the motivation and energy levels up are also part of their responsibilities. They give continuous feedback to strategic leaders and to the visionary leaders. They clearly and transparently communicate operational plans and guide the company in the distribution of rewards and appreciation for individuals and teams. Operational leaders also obtain specific weekly, monthly, quarterly and annual targets and deploy resources for their achievement. Day-to-day problem-solving is an important contribution area for operational leaders. Crisis management is important for them too. The responsibility for daily performance feedback, daily, weekly and monthly closures, analysis of variances, managing the trade, the shop floor, vendors and suppliers and other stakeholders converge at the operational leadership position. Developing or giving inputs to tactical action plans and maintaining records and communication of instructions are also some of their significant responsibilities .

Leadership is widely shared in an organisation and people can lead from any position. Leadership positions occur in all functional and hierarchical sub-systems across organisations. However, there are also leadership positions in the overlapping areas of the sub-systems as one individual can contribute in more than one sub-system at any given time. For example, an individual could substantially contribute in the strategic area as well as the operational area if he has the requisite capabilities. His leadership skills could be many, varied and complex. This means that visionary leaders could do well in the transformational and strategic areas too.

A good example is the chairman of a company who is a visionary leader and also displays competencies in the transformational and strategic areas. However, if he is involved largely in the operational area on a day-to-day basis, people might experience him as highly controlling leader who micro-manages. He may well be perceived as someone who does not provide space for others to work. Ultimately the chairman might be frustrated as he may not have time to think about the strategy of the organisation.

Leaders engaged with organisational transformation and bringing about change in organisations have the courage and the competence to communicate to the top leaders about what they are doing well and where they are going wrong. They also give fair, authentic and mature advice to the top regarding the responses in the organisation and what, how and when course corrections are required. They become internal consultants, coaches and mentors and facilitators.

Some competencies required for leaders:

Leadership competencies for the visionary leader:

1. Managing personal growth and self-development.
2. Taking initiatives and risks.
3. The competency in the area of creativity.
4. The ability to effectively relate.
5. Crafting a vision, communicating it and inspiring others to own and work towards its manifestation.
6. The art of questioning.
7. The ability to listen.
8. The ability to conceptualise.
9. Intuitive competency

Leadership competencies for the transformational leader:

1. Relating effectively with people across the organisation.
2. Perceptual and observation skills.
3. The ability to take risks.

4. The ability to align with the vision of the organisation.
5. The ability to manage power.
6. The ability to communicate properly.
7. Effective negotiation skills.
8. The power and ability to influence.
9. Problem-solving skills.
10. Implementing skills.

Leadership competencies for the strategic leader:

1. The competencies for conceptual, insightful and creative thinking.
2. The ability to align with the multiple contexts of the organisation.
3. To be able to hold multiple and contradictory perspectives.
4. Planning skills for the short and long-term.
5. The ability to connect the dots or systems of thinking.
6. A competitive bent of mind.
7. Managing uncertainty and ambiguity.

Leadership competencies for the operational leader:

1. Clarity about targets to be achieved and results attained.

2. Deep understanding of macro and micro-plans.
3. Planning, organising, monitoring and reviewing skills.
4. Upward and downward feedback.
5. Skills for building standards, processes, procedures, policies and systems
6. Effective communication skills
7. Skills for talent acquisition and retention.
8. Stress-management skills
9. Problem-solving skills.
10. Motivating skills.
11. Time-management skills.
12. Delegation skills.
13. Coaching skills.
14. Multitasking skills.

Operational leaders also have to lead the frontline effectively. Competencies to lead the frontline as understood and observed are:

1. Facilitating them to understand their role with clarity and helping them to focus on important key result areas (KRAs) and the targets to be achieved.

2. The ability to make annual, quarterly, monthly and weekly plans.
3. Working with detailed information and dissemination of relevant information to all the members of the team.
4. Ensuring the timeliness and authenticity of available information.
5. Interpreting trends and patterns from the information for making realistic decisions.
6. Obtaining feedback from the market and the frontline on achievements, processes, enablers, constraints and problems.
7. High need for achieving the numbers committed and ensuring that the right processes are followed for attaining the same.
8. The ability to work with all levels and types of people.
9. The ability to think on one's feet and effectively managing crisis.
10. Organising and monitoring capability
11. High mobility.
12. High energy levels.
13. Time-management skills.
14. Multitasking abilities.
15. Online coaching.

16. Developing juniors and effectively delegating work.
17. The ability to connect the dots and work within the vision to action framework.
18. Putting positive pressure and stretch on team members to excel.
19. The ability to understand in depth the work situation by taking quick reviews.
20. Facilitating the identification of solutions to complicated operational problems that might impede implementation.
21. The ability to understand people with accuracy and keen perceptiveness.
22. Identifying and developing talent.
23. Walking the talk.
24. Personal integrity.
25. Networking with trade, the market and stakeholders in the external environment.
26. The ability to keep the team together.
27. The ability to retain talent, motivate and inspire.
28. Politically astute.
29. Speed in decision-making abilities.
30. Courage to take risks in allocating resources and making unconventional but ethical decisions.

31. Taking accountability on behalf of the team.
32. The ability to continuously learn from past mistakes and successes.
33. Humility in using one's authority and power.
34. Tabling the facts.
35. The ability to effectively relate with peers from other functions.
36. Effective oral and written communication skills.

The areas of envisioning, strategic thinking and planning, transformation and change management which includes the development of people, structures, processes, systems and innovation and translating the vision and plans into action are all significantly important areas for leadership contribution. However, it is important to remember that the focus of leadership behaviour is to bring about major, and at times, radical shifts and change. These changes are of course positive, resulting in growth, quality and service and development levels not experienced before. Together with the results and outcomes, the leadership journey itself is full of learning, passion and inspiration which shapes both competence and character.

Self-Awareness and Self-Management

My lessons in self-awareness and self-management for leadership development have been powerful. I have seen leaders work on themselves as people and have demonstrated great capability for personal transformation. The transformation journey commences when leaders understand their own personal needs and aspirations clearly. They attempt to discover their own sense of purpose and display the courage to define and own it and work towards it. Leaders also demonstrate an uncanny mental strength to own failures, celebrate and reward the self for successes.

At times there is an enhancement of the emotional quotient in leaders, especially when they become aware of their negative and positive feelings and attitudes. This very often is accompanied with the awareness of how the self is evolving and the skill and the courage to perceive the self objectively. There is also an awareness and enhancement of strengths that help leaders manage contradictions and conflicts.

Self-development also includes strengthening our ability to be transparent about perceived self-related strengths and weaknesses and share them with relevant people from whom we can obtain more feedback. Sharing credit and the capability to appreciate the contribution of others is an important milestone in the journey of personal development. The courage to be vulnerable and the ability to be immersed in the service of others and the larger vision is a significant virtue. Personal transformation processes also indicate disciplining oneself and postponing the compulsions for the immediate gratification of needs. Self-management fortifies the person with the competence to manage failures and disappointments. The ability to display equanimity, composure, calm and balance in difficult and trying situations are also strengths that evolve in this journey. Personal transformation also encompasses the ability to manage negative and positive pressures effectively and to keep stretching oneself beyond todays proven strengths and capabilities.

Self in the Leadership Role

There are certain demands from the self in the leadership role. Conversations with many leaders in my career in business operations, HR consulting and in social services has shown that there are changes and developments that take place in the core of the self. A number of leaders experience equanimity and positivity as strong feelings. Visionary leaders harbour a lot of passion and courage in their hearts. Transformational leaders show a child-like curiosity for learning. A number of leaders are giving and also forgiving by nature and do this relentlessly. Operational leaders at the core become focused and tough which facilitates them to manage crisis, constraints and difficulties. Transformational journeys and the self-development stories of a number of leaders indicate their learning in relationship-management and an appreciation of the values of mutual respect, warmth, genuineness and empathy. This helps in developing high self-worth and self-esteem. Perceptiveness and sensitivity to people and the environment and appreciation of others are other important dimensions of leadership behaviour. Visionary and strategic leaders are integrative and inclusive in their approach to work and in their thought processes and have the ability to juxtapose the day-to-day with the big picture. Leadership necessitates the internalisation and the display of authenticity, fairness and humility.

Leadership and Managing Relationships

Leaders create a sense of purpose in others. The larger purpose fits in well with personal goals and aspirations. Alignment with others in the team is around the big picture and the larger purpose, even though personal goals and aspirations of individual team members could be different. Leaders invest time and effort in building meaningful and close relationships. Effective relationships are built on trust and respect. Relationships are founded on and sustained through mutually acceptable and clear expectations and sensitivity.

These relationships facilitate growth and problem-solving and the utilisation of opportunities. Moreover such relationships also help in overcoming stress and difficulty by increasing self-confidence, the willingness to take risks and initiative and provide support for self-expression and creativity. Leaders are also committed to the success of individuals in their team and the team as a whole. They encourage learning and pass on their own knowledge and experiences to the team, thereby assuming the role of mentors and coaches. The relationship encourages communication, authenticity and transparency.

Leadership and Learning

A number of examples and stories of leaders show that they take charge of their own learning. They are curious to know and learn. They are not shy in admitting that they don't know some things and they meet, interact and surround themselves with knowledgeable and experienced people. There are some principles of adult learning which appear to be relevant in the manner in which leaders learn. Adults learn best when:

1. They set their own learning goals and targets.
2. Learning something will help them solve a professional or a personal problem. They also learn well when they are able to enhance their performance at work and become more effective in their family or social roles.
3. They track their progress. Doing this continuously helps adults learn better. When they receive positive or negative feedback from a credible source regarding their performance they strive to learn better too.
4. There is clarity as to why they should learn.

5. There is the freedom to ask questions, clarify doubts and contribute their ideas and experiences in the learning process.
6. Experiential learning and self-learning are more powerful methods for adult learning.

Leaders learn in these major ways:

1. Through introspection or by learning from past successes and failures.
2. Reflection or learning from the present situation that they are in.
3. Learning from new experiences and taking risks to learn. This could also mean learning vicariously and indirectly, absorbing things and letting the subconscious play its role in learning.
4. Leaders also consciously and keenly observe and perceive events and learn from them.
5. Sensitivity helps leaders learn.
6. Leaders use their intuitive capability for learning. Since leaders keep absorbing information consciously and unconsciously and keep being exposed to many new and varied situations they have wide and deep knowledge about a variety of things. This

also helps them make good assumptions. Intuition becomes good with increasing knowledge and experience.

7. All leaders make decisions with incomplete information as information is never complete at a given time. Leaders feel and think through complex situations and also don't hesitate to listen to their gut or intuition.
8. They understand complexity, helped by intuition and sensitivity.
9. Leaders also learn to manage and live with contradictions and ambiguity.

Leadership Development

Leadership development has become a major research, training and a consulting area. Thousands of hours and dollars are being spent in this area every year. Large numbers of people from industries and other organisations including the armed forces are being sponsored for leadership training. Does leadership education and training which is conducted by business schools, trainers and consultants have a meaningful and lasting impact on developing leaders? Do leaders who have made a difference like Bill Gates, Steve Jobs,

Nelson Mandela, Ratan Tata and Mahatma Gandhi get trained in this way? Yes, but largely in many other ways too. So how did they develop as leaders?

Leadership development cannot be outsourced completely to consultants and trainers. Leaders take charge of their own development and there are experiences at the workplace, at home and in social interactions that facilitate the development of leadership behaviour and competencies.

Let's talk about the context or the situations which are conducive for developing leaders.

Leadership competencies develop in situations of work and life which are uncertain, ambiguous and perhaps difficult but definitely full of challenges and opportunities. Examples of this are periods of economic downturn or recession, during which a number of people are challenged and inspired towards self-employment, entrepreneurship or leadng the transformation of large and established organisations.

Difficulties experienced in situations of abject poverty encourage the qualities of resilience and courage to overcome those difficulties which in turn help in nurturing leadership competencies. Early responsibilities which are given both in the family and at the workplace are seen to develop leadership competencies. A child from a poor family often learns the hard way, taking early responsibility and working his way up to economic self-reliance, betterment as he generates wealth for the family.

The story of leadership has a lot to do with responsibility for the self and for others. Self-responsibility could be for education, economic self-reliance, recognising personal talent and working hard to realise one's potential, managing stress, developing professional competencies and succeeding in work.

Responsibility for others could be helping the team to achieve, a work partner to become successful, achieving group targets and organisational goals, taking risks and leading the team with courage to do new things. Taking responsibility for others failures and sharing credit are also a part of this.

Role models who set examples by taking responsibility also help develop this orientation in others. Appreciation for confidence and the initiative to take responsibility encourages the development of leadership behaviours.

When seniors delegate responsibility and authority the opportunities for developing leaders increase. Team members become motivated to assume larger responsibility, own the challenge and mobilise team-work to achieve larger work goals and complete tasks which they have never managed before.

So at the core, leaders develop a willingness to take responsibility and commit time, effort, emotion to see that commitments are upheld and whatever is planned is completed. They also display the need to close and complete undertaken tasks.

Responsibility and commitment create ownership of goals, targets and tasks. Leaders display a high sense of ownership and they take accountability. Developing leadership is not only about training people on skills. Developing a mindset of responsibility, commitment, ownership and accountability is significantly important.

Leaders are therefore people who learn to become responsible, committed and accountable. That seems to be at the core of leadership behaviour. Leaders are confident and proud people and display a high internal locus of control.

How to Develop Responsibility and Accountability?

Many parents and seniors in organisations exert positive pressure in order to make people accountable. They provide space and freedom to take decisions and actions and this goes a long way in creating leadership talent. Relationships in such families and organisations are not dependent and debilitating.

The delegation of authority and responsibility creates responsible and dependable team members.

Choosing one area of work at a time facilitates the emergence of leadership talent. Doubts are dispelled and inconsistencies in behaviour are rectified through timely discussions and feedback. This also improves concentration and motivation to perform at higher levels. . Leaders must be able to manage rest and work in a way that it controls and decreases physical, mental and emotional fatigue so that focus is not obstructed.

The management of ego and arrogance, which sometimes accompanies positional power and authority, might at times create a false sense of superiority and infallibility. Such a person does not like being contradicted and feels he knows all. This decreases one's ability and willingness to listen and after a while people stop communicating, lose interest in providing open and frank feedback and sharing ideas and suggestions for improvements. Fear might lead to an aversion in people for taking risks, remaining in their comfort zone and they may become increasingly complacent and comfortable with the status quo.

Nothing can be more demotivating than the arrogance of leaders. This arrogance can create low self-worth and self-esteem in team members. It is easy to create low self-worth but difficult to reverse it once created. Arrogance is also infectious and is absorbed quickly by people close to such leaders. In other words, people working closely with such leaders also become arrogant. The flip side of arrogance is insecurity. Arrogance is based on a false perception of superiority which is mainly connected with positional power and authority and the license to punish people and instil fear.

It is not easy to manage the arrogance of leaders. Normally the easiest way in which people respond to arrogance is through sycophancy and flattery. People also succumb to the pressure of agreeing with everything that the leader believes or says and disagreements become more and more infrequent in meetings and discussions. This affects the quality of decisions in critical areas, leading to detrimental and damaging actions and decisions.

The process that is negatively impacted is communication—both upwards and downwards. Authenticity of information decreases, leading to ineffective decisions emanating from erroneous and incomplete information which is biased and motivated by personal gains and agendas. An arrogant individual suffers from a superiority complex. The flip side of this complex is an extreme feeling of insecurity which results in feelings of inferiority, low self-esteem and self-worth. When leaders harbour such feelings their behaviour encourages others to hide or distort communication in order that they feel that all is well. False impressions are created and facts and truth are not stated, and therefore, communication loses transparency and openness. If this continues for long, people become complacent and political and the performance of individuals, teams and the organisation is negatively affected.

Arrogant leaders make others feel small, insignificant, and unworthy. With the self-respect of people being damaged, it is difficult to maintain high levels of engagement with work and the organisation. Attrition is one of the indicators of disengagement. Others are lack of interest, initiative, ownership, poor effort and hesitation to assume higher responsibility.

Arrogant leaders create empty and arrogant organisations. The signs of an arrogant organisation are usually both visible and invisible. However, sensitive and perceptive customers, vendors and other stakeholders pick up the messages that speak of arrogance quickly. At the organisational level, some early signals of arrogance are:

1. An unwelcoming attitude at the reception area of an organisation. When guests and

customers are ignored by the company personnel and disrespectfully treated.

2. When members of an organisation do not adhere to time schedules for meeting customers, other stakeholders and guests. This indicates disrespect, high levels of self-importance and discourtesy.
3. Abrasive and rude communication, especially in public.
4. Leaders displaying a prescriptive and instructional style of communicating and interacting.
5. Deliberately ridiculing and ignoring expertise and experience because of personal bias, personal ambition, and insecurity.
6. Narcissistic tendencies demonstrated through phrases like 'I did this' and 'I did that' in communication and only focusing on one's own conveniences.
7. Arrogant senior leaders do not accept feedback on their attitudes and behaviour easily. People are also afraid to give feedback because of a very high possibility of being punished, arousing their anger and later being unfairly treated.

It seems that when senior leaders are arrogant, transformational leaders who are close to them and who are trusted and respected by them are the best people to give them feedback on their arrogance. Transformational leaders, apart from being close, have the advantage of knowing them very well because they are with them in difficult times so they can be blunt and upfront with them. Arrogance cannot usually be handled well by decent, logical and mild behaviour. It has to be confronted strongly, sometimes harshly, highlighting how it is negatively impacting others, the overall work and the reputation of the leader. Extreme arrogance is actually an emotional and a psychological problem.

Arrogance as a syndrome indicates not being in touch with reality because many times the reasons for arrogance are baseless. It could be anchored in high levels of frustration, anger, shame and guilt and arrogance becomes a façade to hide behind these negative feelings. It creates isolation, negatively impacts relationships, as in the long run dealing with arrogance becomes difficult. The partner in a relationship with arrogant people starts feeling neglected and less significant. It also leads to selfishness and self-centeredness. Intellectually, the arrogant individual begins to stagnate because of the deeply ingrained belief that 'I know all'. Therefore the desire to learn through new experiences and also learn from others reduces. Even if the arrogant leader works hard at his or her self-development, there might be a tendency not to share knowledge and interact, discuss and communicate with others. Coaching and developing others is not the forte of arrogant leaders. Arrogance also indicates a strong need to continuously compete with others and the difficulty in accepting the competence and the talent of others. It also reflects the tendency to exaggerate qualities about the self and hold unrealistically positive self -perception.

The self-importance of arrogant leaders might begin to border on narcissism. It could also be a self-obsessive and self-absorbing syndrome. There is a tendency to look down on older people, those who have lower social status or those less well-off financially. The person is a bully, and therefore is subservient to people in authority, more wealthy people or those who are in a position to help. The arrogance syndrome also includes a tendency to be expedient and exploitative in relationships. Arrogance also leads to emotional fragility and these people are easily hurt, sulk at the drop of a hat, do not have resilience and the strength to cope with crisis, failure and disappointment. They could get into a fight without sufficient provocation and can also become depressive. The opposite of arrogance is not humility but a healthy sense of reality and confidence.

A sense of reality is obtained from two main sources—education and experience. Education may not always be formal like academic exposure and qualifications from universities or institutes of learning. Informal education through apprenticeships, mentoring and coaching also help in acquiring confidence and realism. So a lot of learning happens when elders and experts impart knowledge and experience and also share their wisdom about life and skills to deal with both.

Confidence and realism is also gained through assuming responsibility for oneself and for others. Either one learns to swim or he sinks which means that if a person is thrown in the world alone he or she has to make an effort and take the responsibility to survive. Getting knocked out in life and being pushed around also teaches a person the hard realities of the world.

17

Stories

In this section, I am going to write about men and women who are unknown. Their stories contain the secrets of leadership.

It is true that leadership helps evolve processes and behaviours for breaking free. Living shackled, fettered and in bondage is horrible. The most prized possession for a human being is freedom of spirit and mind. The worst bondage is that of helplessness. Leadership processes wage a war against helplessness. The process helps in breaking free from abject penury, guilt or shame, illiteracy, a life of dismal oblivion, the condemnation of caste or class and control and subjugation. People have also freed themselves from their closely held and guarded life scripts and have smashed the burden of their negative destinies. Freedom and leadership are two sides of the same coin. Achievement and success quintessentially bring freedom. The availability of resources is liberating. Leadership ensures the availability of resources and the competence to utilise them well. Resources free time and boost confidence and independence.

Often these learnings are hidden in inconsequential stories where the main protagonist is an unknown name and will always remain so. The first secret of leadership is that name and fame don't matter and have nothing essentially to do with it. Those who break free are those who lead and vice versa. Many poor and illiterate people have achieved this in their lives.

In India, even today, it is difficult to break the shackles of caste and class. It is unfortunate to be born a Dalit or an untouchable and in a low caste. It is very difficult to manage poverty and survive with dignity. Caste and class have deep roots in our psyche. The determinism is real and binding except when a woman is married; then she acquires the caste of her husband and obviously she also becomes a member of the class that she enters after marriage. The conditioning and identification with caste and class happen on a daily basis and through social and political reinforcements which are strong and lasting. Caste and class also have an impact on the psychological make-up of individuals and large sections of the Indian the society. It is equally damaging for the upper castes and classes as it is for the lower. Not only does it erode free thinking, it also creates feelings of inferiority or superiority which are baseless and illogical. We are imprisoned by our own mental construct and the external context. However, there have been men and women who have quietly and without saying too much about it, removed both from their lives. Here is what I would like to share with you.

Manju—She Grew to Lead

Dandi had crossed her 50th year and would often worry about her two daughters who were still unmarried. The eldest was married—she lived in the village and her husband worked on the farm. He was a landless labourer and earned a meagre daily wage. They had a son and a daughter who couldn't attend school because there was no money for their education. Sujata, the eldest daughter, was illiterate and as there was nothing else to do in the village, she began making baskets which fetched some money whenever there was a sale. She never complained because she knew that no one would extend a helping hand and it was pointless telling her mother who herself was in a tight spot.

Dandi used to stay in a small room in the staff quarters of the sprawling Sharma mansion. With great difficulty she had got this job and was grateful to God for being able to stay in the safety and security of a guarded compound with her two growing and rather attractive daughters. The Sharma family was highly educated, very decent and civilised and powerful in the social and political circles in the country. The Sharmas were upper-caste Brahmins, and with great difficulty, Dandi managed to get the job with them, especially because an old aunt of Mr Kailash Sharma, who stayed with them, had vehemently objected to the decision of employing her. Mrs Kanta Sharma, wife of Mr Sharma, was an educated and a broad-minded woman who had overruled her and taken the decision to employ Dandi despite her being a Dalit. The aunt shifted to the portion of the house occupied by Shiv Pratap Sharma, the younger brother. Dandi's daughters were quiet and disciplined girls and were hardly visible outside their home except sometimes in the mornings, when they came to take instructions from their mother about what to cook for lunch. Dandi, it appeared, had strong likes and dislikes about food and was also careful that nothing should be wasted. She encouraged the girls to make do from what was left over after dinner the previous night. During such visits by the girls, Kantaji had noticed them and was impressed by their manners and behaviour. Moreover, she had heard good remarks about the two girls from the other members of the domestic staff.

Manju, Dandi's second daughter, was a tall girl, dark with very long, thick, black and well-oiled hair. She was reticent and kept aloof and was focussed only on the household work. She took extra care of her mother. She had great affection and respect for Dandi and maintained a dignified distance from the other staff families. Manju wasn't friendly, or even on talking terms, with the other girls in that compound. She didn't like the comments that were made on her caste and especially the old aunt of Mr Sharma, who always made it a point to tick her off for touching the furniture or even the plants and trees whenever Manju walked in the direction of the main gate of the mansion. This hurt and humiliated her a lot. Only three days earlier, Manju had plucked a few white *mogra* (white jasmine flower which blossoms in the morning hours) flowers for her puja and by mistake had touched the main branch of the big neem tree on which the clothes of aunt Sharma had been hung for drying. There was a furore in the house as soon as Manju had been spotted by the aunt near the neem tree. Later Manju came to know that the branch was cut off and the chair and the table which had been kept in the inside veranda were also removed, lest she had touched them by mistake. Aunt Sharma also gave away the clothes which were hung outside to the women in the nearby Dalit colony. Manju thought that this was uncalled for and no cruelty could be worse than this. It broke her spirit and also angered her a lot. She didn't mention a word to anyone, even though her mother had started a conversation about it.

Manju cried every night after the incident. She didn't know how else to respond. She knew that her mother would not leave the job at the Sharma's because of the safety and security which it offered for them. Apart from the aunt, who was cantankerous and a sharp-tongued woman, the rest of the family members were decent and kind. Manju understood her family's difficulties and had the practical sense not to disturb the tranquillity of the house. She couldn't do anything about her caste. It was her fate which had brought her into the Dalit community. However, it was difficult for her to accept the untouchability aspect which was attached to her community. She would turn 18 in a couple of months and it had already become too late for her to be admitted to school. Without education and a decent job, she saw a bleak future for herself and this also applied equally for her sister. Her mother, she knew, couldn't afford school fees and no school at this age would give her admission. Getting married was also not a solution because most boys and young men didn't work seriously and whatever they earned, they blew up on alcohol and other bad habits. Alcoholism was rampant amongst the Dalits and that too strong country liquor. With these thoughts, she would fall asleep every night, and felt depressed and helpless for herself, her mother and also for her sister Usha.

Manju began to stay indoors more and didn't leave the immediate precincts of her quarter. She was hardly seen by even the neighbours who would, in passing, tell Dandi that her daughter was becoming rude and anti-social and that she must talk to her or take her to a good doctor in case she was physically or mentally unwell. Dandi would reassure them that there was nothing wrong with Manju and she didn't have time to chit-chat because of the household chores which she managed to a large extent. No one believed her, and with a cynical grin, would say that they were just cautioning her to pay more attention, lest something might go seriously amiss in the future. Nanno, another elderly Dalit lady who had been working with the Sharma's, felt bad for Manju because Dandi had told her about the old aunt and how Manju had felt about the episode. Nanno was very fond of Manju and advised Dandi to look for a nice boy and marry her off so that she could get away from the mansion and begin to lead a normal and happy life.

A full year had passed without much happening except that Manju had become more reticent and aloof and hardly spoke to her mother and even her sister. This had begun to worry Dandi, who decided to take Nanno's advice. Nanno repeated the marriage solution and told Dandi that she would also seriously start looking around and would spread word in the neighbouring Dalit settlements. Ten days later, as Dandi was oiling Manju's hair on a Sunday afternoon, Nanno came and in front of Manju discussed how she had received a message from Shankargarh that her cousin, who had become a widower about five years ago, had agreed to marry Manju. He was childless and lost his wife in an undetected dengue fever. He was very devoted to his wife, worked with the railways and was educated up to the post-graduate level. Most importantly, he had a permanent government job. He wanted a simple girl who would look after the house and his old mother. The only problem was that he was almost 50 years old, but had 10 years, if not more, to retire. Dandi disapproved of the proposal and said that her daughter was in her teens. How could she marry her off to a 50-year-old man who had been married for almost 25 years before? 'Nanno, the age difference is too much. He's more or less my age. How can I marry my daughter off to him?' She said that it could also be possible that he is impotent and therefore childless. The woman is always blamed in these situations. Dandi told Nanno to refrain from saying anything to the family and to close the topic. She was convinced that Manju and Usha would get good grooms when the right time came and that they could easily wait for another year or two.

Manju had overheard the entire conversation. She didn't mention a word to her mother but decided to find out more about the family from Nanno *masi* after taking her into confidence. The next afternoon, Manju told her mother that she wanted a little coconut oil, knowing that Nanno always kept it with her. Taking her mother's permission she walked across to Nanno's house to find out more about the proposal, the family and the man. Nanno was sitting and gossiping with her sister who had brought the proposal from Shankargarh. On seeing Manju, Nanno's sister asked her, 'Is this Manju? She is ordinary-looking and considering her mother's financial condition where will she find a match like Rajesh? He's a gentleman, so well-educated, with good manners and looked after his wife, God bless her soul, so well. He's financially well-off and will be able to also support Dandi and the younger daughter. What is there in age? And who knows for how long anyone will live in this world—it's all to do with good deeds and destiny. Even young people die today with heart attacks and all these new diseases. It will be extremely foolish to refuse such an offer. Manju smiled and asked Nanno for some coconut oil. Nanno was a generous woman and had never refused her anything. Manju knew that she always missed a daughter and she would, twice or thrice a week, rub oil on her body and her hair. She had showered affection on Manju in her own crude way, but never missed telling her how beautiful she was in her youth. Manju couldn't fathom where her beauty lay. She had bad features and was obese but had a wheatish complexion. Maybe she was arrogant about her colour which she thought made her beautiful. She went inside with Nanno to fetch the oil and taking the chance, asked her to tell her more about Rajesh. Nanno looked at her and whispered 'I always knew you were a sensible girl and had the courage to make your own well thought-out decision. Your mother is very simple in these matters and is not at all worldly wise. Just look at the hard work that she does day in and day out. All boys and most families ask for dowries. Can your mother afford a dowry and the expenditure for a lavish wedding? On top of this, boys in our community don't have secure jobs and most drink and have all kinds of habits. I'll find out more about Rajesh and let you know soon. My sister stays in Shankargarh and knows Rajesh's family well. I'll ask her to let us know more about the family and Rajesh. You should be sensible Manju. Where will you get a match like this?'

A week passed and there was no word from Nanno about Rajesh. Manju decided to wait for a couple of days more and in the meanwhile spoke to Usha about it and let her know what she thought about the proposal. Manju thought about the marriage proposal seriously and came to the conclusion that this marriage would solve a number of problems. Her mother's worry about money for the marriage would be solved because according to Nanno, there was no demand from Rajesh and his family. They wanted a quiet affair and were willing to bear the expenses of travel and stay themselves. Dandi would be spending on a simple dinner for 20 people and whatever the costs of the puja and the actual marriage ceremony were, was affordable. Moreover Rajesh was the only child and therefore there was no complication of a big family and its politics. Manju was happy about the fact that he was an educated man and she was sure that he would encourage her education once he came to know that she was keen to study. This was indeed a big attraction for her and Manju saw this as the most significant factor for her to say yes to this proposal.

Usha was quite upset to hear that Manju was not averse to the marriage proposal. She couldn't understand what was wrong with Manju and how she could even consider marrying a man who was about 32 years older. He was their father's age—why was she not bothered by this aspect? When Dandi, Manju and Usha were having their morning tea, Usha told Dandi what Manju thought about the proposal. Dandi heard Usha to the end, and without saying a word, she picked up her cup of tea and walked away till she was under the neem tree, where she sat sipping on it, with her head down in deep thought. When Manju kept her hand on her shoulder she turned around and told her, 'I know, my child. You are thinking about me and your younger sister. If you are okay with it and confident, I'll agree and convey it to Nanno.'

Manju married Rajesh exactly a month after her brief conversation with her mother. She was happy that Rajesh was an educated man and had agreed and encouraged her to go ahead with her plan to educate herself. For Manju, this was the primary reason for agreeing to marry Rajesh. Her marriage was a nondescript affair. There were only a handful of people who attended the ceremony as Dandi didn't have the money to organise an elaborate dinner. She didn't invite the Sharma's, knowing that they wouldn't eat at her place because of the untouchability aspect. She had informed them and had been advised to do a quiet wedding by Kantaji. Dandi gave Manju a saree and a few clothes to her mother-in-law. She presented a shirt and a pair of trousers to Rajesh and he told her not to buy gold for him as he didn't wear any jewellery. Rajesh, along with his mother and Manju, left for Shankargarh the same night. Manju was tired and sad to leave her mother and sister. When she looked at Rajesh and his mother sitting opposite her in the train, for the first time she realised the enormity of the decision which she had made. Her life had completed changed. She didn't even know anything beyond what Nanno *masi* had told her about the man and woman sitting in front of her, with whom she had decided to spend the rest of her life. She had put at stake her entire life and future, not knowing what the actual facts were. She realised that if anything went wrong, she had no one to fall back upon. It was a frightening thought and yet at the same time comforting because she had the opportunity to turn it around to her advantage in her own way and would learn a lot about taking responsibility. With these thoughts in her mind, she fell asleep and woke up early to find herself covered with a shawl. She looked at Rajesh and found a faint, affectionate smile on his face as he asked her to have a cup of tea which he had fetched from the platform. He told her that Shankargarh was just 15 minutes away.

Shankargarh was a small railway-junction town, more like a village, but because of the railway station it had acquired the status of a town with a bus stop, a small cinema hall and a market. As they rode on the rickshaw towards their quarters, Rajesh pointed out his office which was in the premises of the railway station. It was a small office, perhaps not painted for years, with a small green gate and an asbestos sheet roof. Rajesh told Manju that 11 of his colleagues and his boss sat there and that the ticket collectors and the engine drivers of the various trains also frequented the office. His office timings were from 10 AM to 6 PM but he often got late because it depended on the pressure of the work during a particular day. He had worked in the same office for almost 21 years and had 11 years left for retirement. He was fortunate to have worked under good bosses and with decent colleagues and had not faced any problems. His boss trusted him a lot and had also helped him during the illness of his first wife. He quietly informed Manju that he took his lunch to office. These days, his mother prepared his lunch, but as she was growing old it would be nice if Manju would help her in the morning. He was particular about punctuality and hated to reach office late. Manju listened to him with rapt attention.

It was a spacious quarter and neatly maintained. There were two rooms, a kitchen and an attached washroom. There were two verandas, one in front and one at the back. Surprisingly, the house had a big compound and Manju noticed a small kitchen garden at the side, a patch of lawn in front and a tap also near the boundary wall. Manju loved flowers and vegetables and was happy at the thought that she could do a little gardening in her free time. Rajesh took her to his room and showed her the cupboard in which she could keep her clothes and her belongings. She saw a table and a chair and a few books and magazines in the room too.

Gradually Manju found herself settling in comfortably in the new environment. She had always worked hard in her mother's house and had managed practically the entire house. She helped her mother-in-law in the kitchen and was doing the sweeping and mopping of the house from the second day itself. Her mother-in-law was an affectionate and an understanding woman. One sunny morning, after Rajesh had left for office, she called Manju and said 'Are you comfortable in this house? I hope you are not missing your mother and sister too much? We have very meagre means and lead a simple life. Rajesh is also a simple man dedicated to his work. You haven't even spoken to me all these days. Come here. Sit and talk to me about yourself. What are your preferences in food? Rajesh requested me to give you permission to wear salwar kurta. He said that you are so young and will find it easier to work in that and that you would also prefer wearing it.' She looked at Manju and smiled and made her sit so that she could comb her hair. 'Do you know my name? My mother called me Bitto but my name in school was Rani. Do you know I passed my high school in the first division and wanted to study further but then my father met Rajesh's father and liked him a lot and so I got married? My father owned rice mills and lots of land but my father's elder brother gambled and was an alcoholic so the family gradually ran into heavy debt and lost all its wealth. My husband worked with the railways and for 10 years before his death he was in the same office,' she pointed in the direction of Rajesh's office. 'I lost him in a train accident 26 years ago and that's how Rajesh got this job. Well, Rajesh also deserved the job. I got my provident fund, gratuity and other money but couldn't save much as Rajesh spent a lot on the medical treatment of his first wife. She had a hole in her heart and died despite the care that Rajesh took. God bless him, he is a very caring human being with no bad habits. He is pious and respects women a lot. He was telling me that he would like you to study. I can also teach you if you so wish. Only in the beginning of course, because these days you also have so many subjects which we didn't have in our times.' She excused herself and went in to have a nap. Manju thanked her lucky stars for taking the right decision to marry Rajesh. He and his mother were nice people.

Rajesh had not touched Manju since they got married. Manju had noted this but didn't mind it at all. Rajesh came back early that evening and as he entered the house he found his mother and Manju huddled together over a book. His mother was busy teaching Manju English alphabets. He smiled and said, 'You are doing a good deed before your death, Ma. God will be pleased and forgive all your sins. This is nice as all your forgotten learning will come back with this practice. Teaching in any case is a noble thing to do. I like Manju's resolve to learn.' Patting his mother on her back with great affection he took her permission to take Manju out for an early dinner to a small South

Indian restaurant nearby. His mother happily nodded and told Manju not to bother about her food as she would be happy to eat the left-overs from lunch.

Sipping the butter milk Rajesh bent forward and took Manju's hand in his and said with a shy smile 'I don't know how to say this but thought that however clumsily it is said, it has to be said in any case. Almost two months have passed and I have not touched you. It's not that I don't feel like it, but it's just that I don't want to mess around at this stage at all. You are almost 30 years younger. When I first saw you I saw a daughter in you who I craved for, for so many years. I know that this is no reason to marry you. But when I came to know that you wanted to study and make something of your life I decided that if we get married I will give you all the support to ensure that you could realise your dream. For the next 10 years you'll have to be focussed on your studies and pass your private examinations. In these years, you could well become a graduate. I know that my mother will be happy to help and I'll do my best for this to happen. After graduation so many avenues open up. You can sit for competitive examinations and qualify for the IAS or the railways. You could also sit for bank examinations. Actually the world opens up. But in this time if we have a child then your attention will be divided and nothing will be achieved. I hope you will appreciate what I have just said and also agree.' Manju looked at him and nodded and asked him to order food, knowing that he would be hungry as he had missed his snack with tea in the evening. They had a sumptuous meal and also ordered South Indian filter coffee which Manju thought had a wonderful aroma and taste. Manju opened up for the first time with Rajesh and shared the deep hurt which she carried after hearing the comment of the old Sharma aunty. She asked Rajesh as to why she should feel ashamed about the caste or creed that she has been born in. Rajesh's eyes welled up with tears and bending forward he almost whispered to her, 'Do remember that this world is a beautiful place but also very cruel. These days people only respect position, authority and money. Don't become like the rest but never feel weak.'

Manju had found her mentor and guide in Rajesh. Her mother-in-law became her teacher but Rajesh also engaged a tutor for mathematics, English and Hindi. Rajesh began to review her homework and her class outputs on a daily basis and finalised her weekly class schedules. Books and magazines were bought and Rani, her mother-in-law, helped her actively in the kitchen so that she could have free time in the evenings to read and make notes. Manju enjoyed both household work as well as her studies. Lately she cooked different snacks for Rajesh by looking up recipes in her mobile. Both Rani and Rajesh appreciated her culinary skills. Manju felt happy and secure for the first time in her life. Rajesh also shared with her information regarding his salary and savings which made her feel respected.

In the past three months Dandi and Manju had kept in touch, and knowing that Manju had adjusted well in her new environment, Dandi's stress decreased substantially. However, she could not get over the concern of the huge age difference between Rajesh and Manju and was worried about their physical and emotional compatibility. She felt embarrassed asking Manju about this, but decided that after a few months that she would discretely broach the topic. 'Usha,' said Dandi, 'is doing fine and has taken a lot of responsibility of the house.' She was actively looking out for a suitable groom for her too and had spread the word in the community. 'God willing she too will settle down well,' said Dandi and then she would be free from her responsibilities.

Rajesh spent a little money to get the TV repaired and had it installed one evening. His mother thanked him and asked him to take the money spent on repair from her. Manju wondered why he had done this and wasted his money. She was not used to watching television as there wasn't one in their house before she got married. She thanked Rajesh, but on finding time, mentioned this to him so that he did not come under any unnecessary financial strain. She had caught herself lately thinking a lot about Rajesh and also worrying about him. If he got late from office she would constantly keep looking out of the window. For the first time in the last two or three months, she had also noticed that Rajesh was a pleasant-looking man with a trim, attractive physique and he also dressed well. There was a quiet dignity about him and his smile, especially, was very endearing. Did Rajesh like her in a way a man likes a woman, she thought? As soon as this thought crossed her mind she tried to force it out as it was quite useless thinking about it at this stage of her relationship with him.

Rani had cooked *kheer* for lunch on a Sunday afternoon and informed Rajesh and Manju about it. She also told them that she would be happy if both of them could plan a dinner out that evening to celebrate their first wedding anniversary. Manju replied, 'Thanks a lot, Ma, but I think we should stay at home with you and make something which you and Rajesh like for dinner. Let me cook the evening meal and you simply rest. We should not be wasting money like this.

After all it is honest, hard-earned money.' Rani hugged her, kissed her forehead and blessed her. Rajesh said, 'The little girl is becoming wise and responsible. I hope she doesn't become miserly.' Teasing Manju, he asked his mother to handover the saree that he had bought for her. It was a pink and mauve cotton saree, quite attractive and a little expensive too. He had also given one to his mother. Manju was moved by this gesture and thanking him she said, 'I feel very happy in this house and I would like to thank Ma and you for looking after me so well. God has been kind and I consider myself to be very fortunate that I became a member of this family.'

Manju broke down and cried and both Rajesh and his mother consoled her, assured her of their continuous love and support and praised the qualities of her head and heart. Dandi called a little later to wish her. Before ending the conversation she asked, 'When are you planning to start a family? I hope all is well. Is your husband okay? Hope he can give you a child. His first wife didn't have a child. Sometimes the problem is with men. He's getting old and if you delay any longer, it might become a problem. Ask him to get a check-up done.' Manju was lost for words. She ran into her bedroom and her evening was ruined. Rajesh noticed everything and decided to ignore it.

He thought that Manju should learn to fight her own battles. After he was gone she would have to manage a large part of her life alone and become strong and efficacious to do it. He would have to play the role of a mentor, father and husband for her. Not at all an easy combination and therefore he too had a major challenge ahead of him.

A few visits to her mother's house, a full schedule of studies, looking after Rani during and after her two episodes of ill health—once typhoid and the second of dengue—looking after the house and taking care of Rajesh saw three years through for Manju. She had been married for three years and in these years she and her life had entirely changed. She was well-prepared to give a shot at the eighth standard examination which was also conducted for private students by the state boards. Rajesh felt proud of her because she had worked really hard with her tuitions and had proved to be an intelligent and a conscientious student. She had not neglected any other responsibility in the house. He gave personal attention to her mathematics study because he felt that girls generally had a mathematics phobia and so did Manju.

Manju passed the eighth standard examinations with flying colours and she was well into studying for her 10th standard board which were coming in just seven months. Rajesh was also doing well in office. Things at home were fine except Rani's health which played up from time to time. She had become weak but insisted on helping Manju in the kitchen. Her knees began to give her problems and she also had a stiff lower back. She was losing weight rapidly and her appetite was going down. Manju worried about her a lot as she had grown very fond of her and felt that she gave her more support than her own mother had ever given her. Rajesh noticed this and thanked his lucky stars to have found Manju at this stage of his life. The only aspect that concerned him deeply was her young age and the fact that she would miss out on a lot of personal happiness and the pleasures of married life. It would have been different if she were married to a younger man, someone of her age and generation. These days he also introspected on understanding the reasons of taking a decision to marry her. What did he want from this marriage? What actually made him take this decision and why was he feeling guilty and anxious after almost five years of marriage? Was Manju really happy? Did she miss a normal married life? What if she was attracted to a younger man and decided to leave him? After all, she was about to complete her 23 year.

The garden looked beautiful. There was a patch of lawn in front of the house which Manju loved.

It gave her immense satisfaction to water that lawn and keep it free from weeds and any wild, unwanted grass growth. She had also worked hard at the upkeep of the flower beds and the flower pots. There were big and colourful dahlias, pansies, zerbras and flocks in almost all shades of pink and mauve. Her garden was resplendent with colours and fragrance and she was glad that she had the support of Rani and Rajesh for this hobby which was so close to her heart. The vegetable garden was also doing well. She had all the winter vegetables from the vegetable garden and only shopped for potatoes and garlic. Her gingers and tomatoes were also doing well and people couldn't believe that she obtained almost a kilogram of wonderfully healthy and aromatic turmeric from her garden which she had dried and stored in powered form for her cooking. It would last for more than a year for her requirements. Whenever she had a little time from her afternoon and morning studies, she would devote it to the garden.

Her neighbours were decent people. They were all junior staff from the railways or the other government offices in Shankargarh. The area where she lived was safe and secure and neatly maintained. There were trees all over with a park in front where mostly school-going children played in the evenings on weekdays and then throughout the day on Saturdays and Sundays. She had never ventured that side and didn't know anyone in the neighbourhood. She had also seen some young boys and girls and one young man was a frequent visitor to the park in the mornings. He would bring his yoga mat and do rigorous yogic exercises for an hour on a daily basis. He was a good-looking man with a wonderfully attractive physique. Sometimes she found him looking towards her house and watch her work in the garden. He lived in the third house in that row. Lately she had noticed that he came to the park more frequently and that too in the afernoons, sit under a tree and read. Understanding what his interest could be, Manju stopped going to the garden in the afternoons. She would complete the garden work in the morning while Rajesh was at home and requested him to sit and have his morning tea in the garden. They could spend a little time together in the morning in this way. Rajesh understood the reason for the change in timing for the garden work and admired her wisdom and maturity.

Manju did extremely well in the 10th board examinations and obtained admission for her graduation in the local college. She opted for political science and history and Rajesh felt that this combination of subjects would also give her a good grounding for the competitive examinations. She was nearing her 28th birthday when the graduation results were declared. She had topped her college and did extremely well in all the subjects. Rani and Rajesh were jubilant and so were Rajesh's colleagues in his office. They were all praises for his support to Manju and told him that he had set an example for them too. Dandi and Usha's reactions were peculiar. Dandi said, 'What will happen with all this education? There are so many girls who are educated and are still just managing their homes. You've been married for 10 years now and there are no signs of you ever having a child. It will be very difficult for you in the future. I am sure your husband is impotent and that's why his first wife didn't conceive and in grief just passed away. You are still young. Leave him and get married to someone else. In any case, he is nearing 60. He will retire soon and after that who knows about life and death.' Usha married seven years ago and had three children. She came on the phone and said, 'What will you do with a degree? The real degrees are our kids… think about what Ma has just said and take a decision. We are very worried about you.'

Manju was in a state of shock. She had never thought along these lines. She was badly shaken up by the nastiness of her mother and sister. Didn't they understand what Rajesh and her mother-in-law had done for her? Couldn't they see how happy she was and her feeling of both financial and emotional security had increased by leaps and bounds? In the last 10 years her health had also improved. She had a glowing skin, her hair had become stronger, longer and glossier and she looked attractive in her new and elegant sarees and salwar kurtas. She had a comfortable home, and above all, she had found people who respected and loved her and looked after her like a daughter of the house. Lately Rajesh had begun to share all the financial details with her and had also opened a joint account with her. She also had an account with her mother-in-law. Both Rani and Rajesh inquired about what was bothering her while they had tea in the evening. Manju didn't mention anything to Rani but as soon as she was alone with Rajesh in their room she broke down and shared with him all that she had heard from her mother and Usha. She had not complained about Dandi and Usha before this to Rajesh.

He held her close to his chest and whispered 'Who says that you won't have children? Of course we'll have children. I want a daughter exactly like you, beautiful, loving and talented. We'll wait for another two years till you study hard and clear your competitive examinations and start your work as an IAS officer. I'll be the proudest husband in this world. Ma will also be so happy. It will be a solid achievement for you. You have so much patience. And please understand it has been very difficult for me to stay away from you. I didn't want you to lose this happy period of your childhood which you didn't experience at your mother's home. I know what a happy childhood contributes to in life. I had one and value it a lot. My father showered all his love on me till he was alive. He made me what I am today and my mother also had a role to play in this.' He caressed Manju as she cried in his arms.

Manju decided to do her teacher's training as she always wanted to teach and had plans to study further. Rani encouraged her to follow her heart. She did well in her B.Ed. examination and immediately got a job in a girl's school in Shankargarh to teach in the primary section. Rajesh and Rani consulted her and then took a decision to employ a maid for sweeping and mopping the house and to clean the utensils. Manju insisted on managing the entirety of the cooking so that there was no strain on her mother-in-law. She would leave for school at seven in the morning and it took her less than 20 minutes to reach. She was back at half past one in the afternoon, well in time to give Rani her lunch, with piping hot rotis. The arrangement worked beautifully. The principal received very good feedback on Manju from the parents, the students and the staff. In no time she became popular amongst the students and began playing an active role in co-curricular activities too. She discovered and so did the others in school, her leadership capabilities and began to be roped in projects and functions which required supervising and leading groups of students and also handling the staff members. What people admired was her hard work together with her capability to focus, communicate and maintain discipline. She was a determined soul and would not give up until she had completed a task.

Two years passed very quickly and Rajesh was on the verge of retirement. He looked a bit lost and depressed and had become quiet. Rani too was worried and had shared her thoughts with Manju. The office threw a decent farewell for Rajesh. The team praised Rajesh's qualities of head and heart and said that in hard work and punctuality, he stood out as a great example for his juniors. His team gave him a shawl and a silver plate. He retired after a service of almost 35 years. While returning home, he looked at Manju and said, 'Now my time is all yours, madam. We'll do a number of things together. Things that you and I wanted to do for a very long time.' In the next three years, in rather a quick, if not hurried succession, Manju had a son and a daughter. The pregnancies were difficult and during her daughter's time, she went through a complicated operation that was almost touch and go.

Dandi had been ailing for a number of years and lately had expressed the desire to see Manju's children. Rajesh advised Manju to break her silence and call her mother and then go with the children and spend a few days with her. Manju relented and travelled to her mother's place during the winter vacations when her school was closed and the children also had their Christmas holidays. She was pained to see Dandi after a number of years. The children were meeting their maternal grandmother for the first time. Gaurav was almost 10 and Garima was eight and a half. Dandi was very happy to see Manju looking well and was relieved to see her with the kids. Nanno *masi* had aged and couldn't walk. She was on a semi-retirement from the mansion job and would only go in the evenings to supervise the cleaning in the wing occupied by Kanta Sharma. Nanno showered a lot of affection on the children and told Manju, 'It was the wisest decision that you took. I am very happy to see you grow and achieve. You also have wonderful children. I must say that they are very well brought up.'

Manju returned from her mother's place feeling a little disappointed. Dandi didn't seem to be very happy and most of the time Manju felt a resentment against Rajesh and Rani. She was also continuously comparing her with Usha. Well, such was life and she had to accept it. She decided to cut short her stay and returned home on the pretext that the school examinations were just round the corner and she had a number of things to manage and organise on the home front. Rajesh sensed her unhappiness and encouraged her to come back.

Rani was helping Manju in the kitchen as the maid had taken a few days leave. She couldn't do much because of an excruciating pain in her left knee. Manju noticed her discomfort and rubbed a pain-relieving balm at night. Rani was touched by Manju's care and concern and blessed her silently. Rajesh, on the breakfast table announced his decision to start giving tuitions to students in mathematics and all the science subjects, but said he would keep a way from Manju's school as it would, on principle, not be the right thing to do. He also decided to go back to studying and planned to do another masters in physics which he was fond of and always secured high marks in the subject. In no time, Rajesh had 10 students coming to him. He chose afternoon hours because the house work and lunch were over and the children, after school, also went out to play. Manju and Rani always had an hour's afternoon nap and therefore they were also not disturbed. In the evening hours, when Manju prepared dinner and the children got busy with their homework, Rajesh found time to study. He had contacted a retired professor of physics, Mr Raveen Gupta, who agreed to guide him in his studies. Maya, the maid, resumed her duties after 10 days. It was a big relief for Manju.

Rani's health was deteriorating as she was about to touch 80 in a couple of months. Her appetite had become half of what it used to be and she was rapidly losing weight. She also had night shivers and was irritable. Manju asked Rajesh to have her full health check-up done in a nearby health clinic which had a good reputation. She was diagnosed with a thyroid problem and fluctuating blood pressure. She always had more salt in her food and was also fond of pickles and spices. Manju decided to take extra care of her as she was very dear to her. She would cook lotus stems for her every second day as it was rich in iodine and controlled her intake of salt and red meat. She was not a big meat-eater but enjoyed her mutton curries. In no time, Rani looked better and with the thyroid medication, her weight also came back gradually.

However, it was difficult to keep her away from spices and pickles. Rani had great recipes for a variety of pickles which she would make every summer for the whole year. She also made the most aromatic and tangy pickle from carrots, beetroots and turnips, using a lot of mustard seeds and mustard oil. Rajesh simply loved it and ate it throughout the winter months.

Time just flew by and soon Gaurav and reached the 10th standard. Garima was doing well in the eighth standard. Both the children were bright and diligent and also were active in co-curricular activities. They were very proud of their mother who had graduated to the secondary school and was the class teacher of the seventh standard. She had also been given a major charge of the school administration. Both students and teachers spoke extremely well of her and a number of parents simply doted on her. One day the school bus didn't come and so Rajesh decided to drop Manju and the children on his scooter. As the children reached the school gate their classmates, who were standing in a group, greeted Manju and tentatively wished good morning to Rajesh. They saw Rajesh for the first time. As Manju took a few steps towards the main building she heard a boy who studied with Gaurav say, 'I didn't know that your grandfather also stayed with you. Very impressive *yaar*, even at this age he has the courage to drop all three of you on a scooter. He looks quite fit for his age. By the way, what does your father do and where does he stay?' Gaurav and Garima didn't respond to the questions and looked quite embarrassed.

Manju sat with the children after school and talked to them about the comment about Rajesh which she had heard near the gate in the morning. She said, 'It's true that your father is 30 years older and marrying with such an age gap is not a normal thing to do. Please realise that your father's and my life were not normal. He battled for almost 20 years with an ailing wife and really looked after her well. I belonged to a very poor family and was completely uneducated till I was 18. We belong to the Dalit community and as children we were badly treated as untouchables. You can't imagine the humiliation that I suffered. Therefore I decided to marry your father, educate myself, stand on my own feet and get away from the Sharma mansion. Rajesh and I got married and your father and grandmother encouraged me to study and supported me in all possible ways. Today whatever I have achieved is because of them. Yes, your father is above 70 years but see what he is doing. He still keeps himself busy and is earning. He's also doing a noble thing by teaching young boys and grooming them for the future. You should be proud of him. Gaurav should spend a lot of time with him in order to learn, make him feel wanted and you both should realise that these are precious years with him because he is not going to outlast me. I know that I will lose him and I shudder at that thought.'

After a couple of days Manju saw the kids playing carom with Rajesh before dinner. It was such a happy feeling to see a growing son laugh and play with his father and trying to develop a bond which was not visible before. Rajesh and Manju took the children to see a few Dalit settlements nearby just to make them understand how young Dalit men lived. They met a few families and heard the stories of domestic violence and alcoholism which were heart wrenching. Both Gaurav and Garima saw the plight of the children and the conditions in which they lived. It was an eye-opener for the kids and for the first time they felt deep respect and regard for their father, Rajesh Shankar. He had dropped his surname and had adopted Shankar instead because his father felt that it would be best that in school he was not identified as a Dalit.

Shankargarh was reeling under a cold wave and the prediction was that the temperatures would dip further. Rani had a dry cough, the sound of which was very disconcerting and worrying. Manju had asked her mother-in-law to show herself to the doctor but she had declined the suggestion saying, 'Oh it is because of the cold. I'll be okay with your ginger tea and a few gargles before I sleep at night. I've also kept cloves and pepper corn near my bed side and pop in a few at night. Don't worry about me. You already have too much on your head. God bless you.'

Manju had cleaned up the kitchen after dinner. The children had gone to bed and Rajesh was in the room, tucked in bed with a book. Manju felt tired and a little depressed. The comment in school still hurt her and the look in the eyes of the children while she explained to them Rajesh's situation, kept coming back whenever she was alone. She made a cup of tea for herself and sipping it quietly, sank into the chair in the living room. As the family grew, they needed more space, therefore they had constructed another room which had become a living and an all-purpose room. She looked out of the window and saw a velvety black, clear sky with a few bright stars sprinkled which were emitting a wonderfully blended silver and gold light. She had lived for more than 25 years in this house. The house, the surroundings and the family had become an integral part of her existence. Tears began to stream down her cheeks. She sat there for almost an hour and then thought that she would go to Rani's room to see how she was and would give her an additional blanket if she needed one.

She tiptoed into the room and touched her mother-in-law gently and asked her, 'Ma, do you need another blanket? In any case, I'll give you one so that you are comfortable during the night. It is bitterly cold.' There was no response from Rani. Manju looked at her as she covered her and moved closer towards her. There was a deathly silence in the room and Manju's heart missed a beat. She sensed that there was something seriously amiss and moving very close, she put her hand on her chest and called out to her. There was no movement and response. Manju panicked and ran out of the room to tell Rajesh. The children also woke up and all four were in Rani's room, rubbing her foot and turning her and wanting her to respond. Rajesh rushed out of the house, started his scooter and within 30 minutes was back with Dr Amit Pandey, who declared that Rani had passed away almost an hour back. She had the string of brown beads in her right hand and Dr Pandey said that it appeared she passed away in prayer. What a wonderful way to go at the age of 91. She was 18 when Rajesh was born. The children were inconsolable and Rajesh maintained a stoic silence. It was a dignified funeral, befitting a woman who had led and nurtured a family with courage, wisdom and affection. Manju lost a mother and a companion. She knew that her world would not be the same any more. The 13th day puja was performed in detail and Rajesh and Manju went to a school for orphans and organised lunch and distributed clothes her memory.

She was a great believer in education and she encouraged Manju's education too, not leaving any stone unturned so that her daughter-in-law could forge ahead with her graduation and teacher's training. Manju had a big picture of Rani framed and placed in the living room. She would put flowers every day beneath the picture and light incense. For her, Rani was the epitome of a mother's unconditional love and support.

The love and companionship between Rajesh and the children grew and they virtually became an inseparable threesome. Manju was very happy to see the respect and love between them. However, she also worried a lot about Rajesh's health. She knew that if anything happened to him the children would not be able to take the blow. Gaurav had become very close to him. Rajesh was his mentor, confidante and his pillar of strength. Rajesh was almost 75, his birthday was fast approaching and she, with the children, was planning a small party at home. It would be the first time that they would be inviting people over for a meal. She had to be strong and not let her fears negatively influence the kids and spoil these happy years. Gaurav, it appeared, had read her mind because after returning from school he walked into her room and said, 'Ma, dad's birthday is just six weeks away. We must start planning for it. I know that because of granny we cannot and should not have a loud and grand show. However, a 75th birthday is very significant and therefore we must celebrate it well. Let Garima also give her ideas and one evening all three of us must sit and plan it.' Manju said that he was absolutely right because time would fly as it usually did when people kept busy from morning till the evening. Garima came in and suggested that the first thing that they should do was to make the guest list because all depended on who and how many people would attend. Manju and Gaurav agreed with her suggestion and it was decided that they would make their own lists and then sit the next evening to finalise one list.

Dandi spoke to Manju when Rani passed away but there was no call from Usha. This Manju found very strange because it was customary to make at least one call for condolence when a near and dear one passed away and Usha knew how close Rani and Manju were to one another. From the kitchen, Manju heard her mobile ringing and leaving the kitchen she called Garima to manage the cooking while she took the call. It was Usha, calling after a number of months. Manju's first thought went to Dandi and she was scared that something must have happened with her and therefore Usha was calling to break the news. It was nothing like that and Manju heaved a sigh of relief. Usha said, 'I thought I would call you and have a chat to find out how you all are doing. It's been very long and we don't get time at all from the household responsibilities. And then of course the examinations of the children. How are your children faring?' She didn't say a word about Rani. Manju said, 'Everything is just fine. The children are doing well and life goes on as usual.' Usha then said something very strange and hurtful and Manju understood what her actual motive behind calling was.

'Oh my, now all your family matters must have settled. I believe your mother-in-law left a substantial amount of money. I must say, you handled her very diplomatically. Even Nanno *masi* was saying that she was very happy with you and had planned to leave a lot of money for you in her will. You always plan things very well. By marrying Rajesh you actually assured a safe and secure future for yourself and your children. When he goes, I am sure he'll also leave lots for you.

After all, he had a financially secure government job. Okay then. At least I have you to fall back on if I need some financial help.'

For days Manju reeled under the shock of her conversation with Usha. She told herself that she would save herself much pain if she stopped analysing the conversation and its various connotations. Ironically, only one's kith and kin, the near and dear ones, can cause this kind of pain. Outsiders are more empathetic and supportive, both in good and bad times. Manju decided not to relate the conversation to anyone because she concluded that some burdens we had to carry ourselves. Rajesh and the children had not done anything to deserve this unhappiness and hurt. She decided to keep away from Usha and not mention this to Dandi.

Manju, Gaurav and Garima did the cooking for three days, mainly at night when Rajesh was fast asleep. Finally, after a lot of discussion and debate, a motley group of people were invited. Some from Manju's school, some from the staff who were close to her, old friends of Rajesh's from the office and some local friends from Shankargarh, people who were also known to Rajesh's parents. Gaurav and Garima invited a few good friends from school and it all totalled to about 20 people. Invitations had been extended and they were told that it was a celebration for Rajesh's birthday. They were also requested not to bring any gifts except flowers because Rajesh was very careful about this. He didn't accept any personal gifts, not even from his parents when they were alive. Everything apart from his pension that he received from his parents, he gave Manju and also nominated his children, giving them an equal share.

Rajesh enjoyed himself thoroughly during his birthday dinner. Everyone seemed very comfortable, relaxed and happy. Manju had prepared an excellent meal and Gaurav, for the first time, realised what it took to cook a good and elaborate meal. He gave full marks to his mother for her menu-planning and the quality and the presentation of the food. Rajesh thanked his family and when the children fell asleep he put his head in Manju's lap and said, 'I didn't know that God will compensate for the grief that he gave me for so many years. I feel blessed to have a life partner like you.'

Manju had been noticing Gaurav's long telephone conversations and she wondered who the girl was. He was still too young to have a serious relationship and then his board examinations were just round the corner. He could not afford to be completely distracted. She watched and waited for a few days and then she decided to speak to him about this. One evening she found him alone and sat with him and said, 'Who is the girl you keep having these very long conversations with? I am worried about you. I have realised that if you go on with this then you won't realise how much time you have spent chatting with your friend. Time you could have devoted to your examination preparation. Please understand that admissions in good colleges are very difficult. You must have a high percentage to reach the cut-off in any case. Who is this girl and what is her name?'

'She studies with me. You must have seen her many times. She is the one who excels in all the co-curricular activities and also gave the classical music recital last year during the annual day celebrations,' said Gaurav.

'Oh I remember. Is she Radhika? I remember her name strangely,' said Manju.

'Yes, Ma. She has been my best friend for almost nine years now. We share a lot of common interests and have great affection and respect for each other. She is a very nice girl and is very understanding, hard-working and balanced, somewhat like you. I can't imagine my life without her. I know it is too early to talk about this but we both feel that if God is kind and if we are together like this for another five to seven years, then we would like to spend the rest of our lives together. Please don't be upset. I wouldn't let all this impact my examination performance.'.

'Oh I didn't realise that you have grown so big as to be able to think about all this. Okay okay, we'll see later. Just concentrate on your studies at the moment. By the way, what is her full name?'

'She is Radhika Purohit Sharma. It's a rather longish surname. I don't know why she has to write such a weirdly long surname. But both her father and her brother insist on it.'

'Is her father Mr Dayanand Sharma, our MP from Shankargarh.?'

'Yes, Ma. Her family has been in politics for generation. She lives in that sprawling *haveli* (large mansion) and hates staying there. It's full of people all the time and she says that there are hoards and hoards of distant relatives who have made the *haveli* their *dharamshala* (a house where travellers and needy people are given shelter).'

Manju was dumbstruck. This was the last thing that should have happened to Rajesh and their peaceful life. She knew that if this friendship continued, there would be nothing else but major trouble. Dayanand Sharma's wife was the younger sister of Kanta Sharma. She had to speak about this to Rajesh and under no circumstances they could allow this friendship to continue, become stronger and later let it culminate in a marriage. That seemed to be in the mind of Gaurav and this was what she had concluded from his description of his relationship with Radhika Sharma. Hell would break lose on all fronts if this relationship continued and became known to people. Manju was very worried and not saying a word to Gaurav, got up and left the room.

She couldn't concentrate in school at all and felt extremely helpless. She relived the time when the old Sharma aunty had told her not to touch the furniture and even the neem tree because she was a Dalit and an untouchable. She would not let this happen to Gaurav and no one in the world would hurt him by condemning him because he was a Dalit, not on her watch. How would the Sharmas respond once they got to know about this friendship? She was certain that they would protect Radhika and persecute Gaurav. They could also physically and psychologically harm him and create immense problems for Rajesh too. She felt unwell in school and wrote a note to the principal to grant her half day's leave. After lunch, Manju went to Gaurav's class to tell him that she was going home because she was not feeling well. As she entered his class, she found him with Radhika. They were studying something and looked very happy together.

She was a beautiful girl and seeing her Radhika got up, came forward and touched her feet. Manju saw the glimpse of a strong and determined man in her 17-year-old son in those few moments. As she left them, her heart told her that Rajesh and she had no business standing in the way of their happiness.

Manju decided to ignore the Gaurav issue for some time except that at the right time she would have to tell him that he should be careful with his telephone calls to Radhika. It was necessary that they both did well in their examinations. She decided not to mention it to Rajesh for some more time, as it was too early to talk about it. As Gaurav became older and more mature he will have to move out of Shankargarh and get exposed to the world. Thus, she thought, might make Gaurav change his mind and the distance from Radhika could help. Radhika could also have a change of heart. Anything could happen, so it would be wise to wait and watch.

Tucking these thoughts away in her mind, Manju got back to her normal school responsibilities and household chores. However, the problem kept surfacing in her thoughts and continued to play on her mind. She was about to enter class when she felt a shooting pain behind her neck and vertigo. She sat down to recover and thought that this could have happened because she had got up suddenly and with a jerk. As she tried getting up the second time, her head spun badly and catching the arm of the chair to gain balance, she sat down and put her head on the table. This time the pain spread to the right side of her neck and began to travel rapidly down to the chest on the left side. She felt like throwing up and also broke out into a cold sweat. Calling out to a few students outside the staff room, she asked them to contact her son. Gaurav ran in a few minutes later and seeing her condition panicked a bit and asked a few of his friends to organise a vehicle to rush her to hospital.

The doctors diagnosed a definite case of angina, a heart condition. They were not very sure whether there was a minor heart infarction or not. They suggested that she be shifted to Lucknow so that in a bigger hospital, with the right diagnosis, proper medication could begin. In Lucknow, Manju was diagnosed with angina and a minor heart infarction. The doctors advised her to rest and hoped that with medication, a change in food habits and more rest and less stress, she could recover. However, it was definitely the first episode and could not be repeated because if it were to occur again, it could cause serious damage to the heart and result in a condition which could go out of control. The doctors separately explained to Rajesh what Manju and the family need to do to look after her health. She was discharged from hospital a week later and was advised rest for at least 10 days.

Rajesh and the children were very worried about Manju's health. The doctor had told Rajesh that these episodes were largely on account of worry, anxiety and stress. All adults, and even children these days, must cope with stress because of the day-to-day pressures of life. Yes, for both Manju and him, life even after marriage had not been easy. So many years of waiting for a normal husband-and-wife relationship between them and the anxiety of the major difference in their age could well be a source of anxiety. Then of completing her education, looking after Rani and bringing up the children with the responsibility and the physical strain of running the house could also be a source of stress. However, of late, what was worrying her? Rajesh didn't have an answer and decided that he would find the right time and speak to her.

After her heart episode Manju found Gaurav not wasting hours and hours speaking on the telephone. He was visibly putting in more effort towards his studies which gave Manju a lot of relief. Garima cared for her like a mother would care for her daughter in ill-health. It is not surprising to see role reversals in situations like these, especially when children are well brought up with the right values and attitudes and a sense of responsibility. Manju had resumed her school duties and according to the advice of the doctors, was taking things a little easy even at school. The school administration, the staff and students were extremely supportive and caring. Manju was praying every day for Gaurav to find another girl who would love and care for him. She wanted him to get over Radhika Sharma as she was convinced that once the girl's family got to know about this friendship, frenzy would be let loose and would destroy the peace and life of their family. Moreover Rajesh, past 75, was not at an age to bear the brunt of these political and social onslaughts. Who knew how he would react when and if he got to know about this friendship. Firstly, he would tell Gaurav that at his age romance was the last thing that he should be wasting his precious time on. His whole life was in front of him and the next 10 years were going to be very crucial to his career and future. When the time came, all that was supposed to happen would happen. Rajesh, in these matters, was a very cut and dry person and Manju was sure that he would brook no nonsense from Gaurav.

Gaurav and Garima did very well in their board examinations. Gaurav topped his class and Manju was very proud of him. Gaurav planned to do his medicine, and motivated by his results, he plunged into the preparation of pre-medical tests. Garima still had two years left for her final board examinations. She had made up her mind to graduate in political science and then sit for the IAS examinations.

Radhika had not done too well. Her parents were extremely disappointed, especially her father, who had dreams about her to finally enter politics or sit for the IAS. Her family was very powerful and position-conscious and also prided themselves for being high class Brahmins. Her grandfather had made a name for himself as a leading lawyer and also amassed large amounts of wealth through his thriving legal practice. Radhika had suddenly come under camera and scrutiny of her ambitious father. Dayanand Sharma, who told his wife Rukmini, 'What have you been doing all these years with this girl? She appears to be distracted and at this rate I'll have to find a groom for her and marry her off soon. If she doesn't do well in her graduation it will be pointless wasting money and time and even good matches will not keep waiting for long. She is also plain-looking, more like her mother's side. My sisters and mother are good-looking aristocratic women. You better do something about her.' Rukmini listened to him quietly and was pained to think that her husband was bound to find a groom like him for the daughter. She would suffer all her life as she had after marriage. Dayanand began to spread the word about his plans to marry Radhika among his friends and relatives, especially in the powerful political circles, hoping to find a family with connections and money.

Rajesh walked into the kitchen while Manju was cooking. It was a pleasant evening with the monsoons just setting in. There was a lovely fragrance of the *mogras* and the *raat ki rani* or the night flowering jasmine which Manju had nurtured with a lot of care and meticulous effort. The trees were lush and swung in the light evening breeze, duly washed and fresh. Rajesh complimented Manju for her wonderful culinary skills and noticed that she always prepared a dish which he liked. He had started walking regularly as he was putting on weight around his waist and knew that if he was complacent he would soon develop a paunch. Manju looked up and asked, 'What's the matter? You hardly visit the kitchen. Is there something that you want?' Rajesh hurriedly said, 'No, I just came to request a little time from you. I want to speak with you about something which has been troubling me for a couple of weeks.' He left the kitchen to respond to his mobile phone which had started ringing incessantly in the adjacent room.

Manju wrapped up the kitchen work, washed her hands and face and brushed her hair—an evening ritual—and settling the pleats of her saree, emerged from the bedroom and sat next to Rajesh. 'Can we talk?' Rajesh, clearing his throat and a little hesitatingly said, 'What has been worrying you or causing stress? I want you to be absolutely frank with me. We are husband and wife and we must be together in everything. Even if I am upset I can assure you that I can handle issues with immense maturity and balance. You have ample evidence of that in the years that we have been together.'

Rajesh listened to her with rapt attention. After Manju related all the little incidents that had taken place regarding Gaurav and Radhika, her background and the impending trouble which she perceived in the future if this friendship continued, she couldn't help but say, 'Is being a Dalit such a crime that young, innocent children and even young men and women will be punished for something which is not in their control at all?' Rajesh surprisingly, was extremely calm, a little amused and didn't look angry or disapproving. He said, 'Manju, Gaurav should not lose focus from his education. His results indicate that he has his head on his shoulders and his feet on the ground. I would also expect the same approach in the next four or five years. Then once he completes his medicine from AFMC (Armed Forces Medical College), Pune which he has managed to be part of entirely on his own steam, no one in the world can stop him and Radhika from getting married if they still wish to do so. There is nothing to get worried about at all. Radhika has to fight her battles with her family and I am sure she will emerge successful as she is a confident young lady.'

Manju was absolutely flabbergasted at Rajesh's response. She had expected him to flare up and lose his cool. Manju then thought of mentioning the caste factor and how it could lead to serious complications with the Sharmas. She said, 'I hope you realise that Dayanand Sharma is a Brahmin and once he knows that his daughter is involved with a Dalit his reaction may be violent. Caste is still a big issue in this country. It is ingrained in our thinking, our identity and behaviour very largely and still dominates our mindsets. Do you understand the social and political enormity of this issue?'

Rajesh in his usual calm and controlled manner said, 'Yes, I do. I know a lot about Dayanand Sharma's family, their likes and dislikes, which I am sure you won't be aware of. I don't particularly like the man and his family. However, we should like Radhika and not let our negative thoughts of what might happen colour our perception and understanding of the fact that both Gaurav and Radhika like or love each other and this has nothing to do with anyone else but them. We are only instrumental in bringing them into the world physically. We don't know why they were born to us or about their destiny. We have no control over their lives and future. That's the simple truth which all wise and good people must accept. It is also not wise to brood over these issues and make yourself sick with high blood pressure.' For the first time in her married life, Manju saw this side of Rajesh. Her admiration for Rajesh increased a hundred fold. She felt much relieved and was certain that Rajesh could manage the issue if at all it happened in the future. Who knew about the future anyway?

Manju quietly learnt a number of lessons in leadership. In Rajesh, she found someone who could take control of his emotions and biases and had immense patience. He did everything very quietly without raising any alarms and led the family into well-reasoned and wise decisions. He would not be negatively critical and hated discussing people and indulging in gossip. He gave respect and therefore earned respect. Even with the children and their young friends, his relations and interactions were respectful and restrained and he showed affection and genuine care. Manju, on the other hand, was mighty courageous and determined for a woman but had the tendency to take too much responsibility and then buckle under pressure. She had to understand that there were a number of uncontrollable factors in life and we had to move away so that situations could play themselves out as they were intended to. It was necessary to give space and to let go.

Dandi passed away in her sleep at the age of 89. Rajesh and Manju were in the Sharma mansion for almost 11 days. The house had to be wound up. One more chapter closed, and Manju was convinced that after this, she would not be meeting Usha ever again. Usha, being her usual self was rude and nasty whenever she got an opportunity. She spent a lot of time with Nanno *masi* and only had unpleasant discussions with Manju over the division of whatever Dandi left behind. Kanta Sharma gifted a silver plate every Diwali to her domestic staff. Dandi had collected twelve plates and had hidden them in the big, wooden container which she used for storing large quantities of rice. The plates lay buried under the rice and Manju discovered them by accident. A few plates looked larger than the rest and Manju suggested to Usha that they divide them in equal numbers and sizes. Usha, however, insisted that they be weighed and costed at a silver jewellery and utensils shop. Rajesh refused to get involved in this onerous task. Manju had to spend two full days getting it sorted out. She let Usha decide which plates she wanted to keep. Manju wanted the task to get over as soon as possible. It was difficult to imagine how two sisters could be so different, having been exposed to the same family dynamics and the same social milieu. However, this was the difficulty as well as the beauty of human life. The struggles and the difficulties in life gave a lot of pain but also provided a lot of learning opportunities.

Rajesh and Manju returned home to find Gaurav and Garima having an intense discussion on politics and current affairs. Rajesh was astonished to hear their discussion which was deep and well-informed. He realised how time had flown and how his precious kids had grown up and were gradually preparing to fly out of the nest. He hoped that he and Manju had equipped them with all the where withal that was needed to face the world. Manju was delighted to see Gaurav back for his holidays. He had done well in his internal examinations in the medical college and was gaining a good reputation amongst the staff and students. She would be proud to see him qualify as a doctor, thought Manju to herself. However, as soon as she saw Gaurav, those words Usha had uttered with so much nastiness during the division of the silverware came back to her and began troubling her. Usha had said, 'You don't need the money now as your son will become a doctor. And I believe he is also planning on marrying a girl from a rich and well-connected family. These days anything can happen. Boys, even while studying in school, think about marriage. This is an age to study and play and not do all this.' Manju had just heard the remark and knew how she must have got to know about Radhika. She was sure that Nanno *masi* had heard some talk in the Sharma mansion which she must have passed on to Usha. Manju thought it best to ignore the remark and even kept Rajesh away from this gossip. She was certain that Gaurav would meet Radhika and keep his relationship with her alive.

Being his mother, she knew him too well. He was a responsible boy and would never let Radhika down. He was very attached to her and also had a lot of respect for her. Manju also knew that Rajesh would support him in taking this relationship forward and marry him off after he had completed his studies and could afford a wife and a family. She was not keen on this marriage because her major concern was Gaurav's safety and she knew that Dayanand Sharma would do his best not to let this marriage take place. For Dayanand Sharma, it was completely unacceptable to give his daughter away to the Dalit community. He himself would be ostracised from his Brahmin society and he had three children to marry off after Radhika, two sons and one daughter, who was the youngest amongst the four. She was also the prettiest and had already received proposals from rich, powerful and politically very well-connected families. If these connections happened through marriage, it would be a big boost for his own, and later for his two sons', political careers. After all, Manju was the daughter of the Dalit maid servant in the Sharma mansion. How could he accept the marriage of his daughter into the family of a maid, and that too a Dalit maid.

Dayanand had observed Radhika leave the house early and return late from college. This happened on a daily basis. He was certain that something was happening and instructed Shastri, his man Friday to find out what the matter was behind these long hours away from home. After a couple of days, Shastri reported that Radhika was spending time with Gaurav who was in town for his holidays from AFMC. He also informed him that Radhika used to visit his parents and spend time with the family over lunches and dinners. Dayanand decided to visit Gaurav's parents and confront them with dire consequences if they encouraged Radhika in any way. He decided to inform his sons, who had completed their graduation and were now helping him in his party activities and meetings.

On a bright Sunday morning, Rajesh had planned to prepare lunch for the children, at least the main dishes, and had requested Garima to make the dal and the rice. They didn't want Manju to enter the kitchen at all and take complete rest and organise her clothes and her room. Manju had put on some music and looked happy and relaxed. Rajesh was also quiet, excited about the meal being prepared and was convinced that the children would love the chicken preparation. Gaurav had gone out shopping with Radhika as he had to replenish his wardrobe with a few warm clothes and relied a lot on Radhika's taste. Radhika loved the chicken curry which was prepared in their house and planned to stay back for lunch. Even though her family were strict vegetarians, she and her brothers ate out and relished chicken, mutton and fish preparations. She couldn't eat pork which Gaurav loved. He had also picked up taste for Maharashtrian food and the Goan style cooking.

The family, along with Radhika, sat down for lunch and were halfway through when the bell rang. Rajesh got up to open the door and said, 'Who would come at this time on a Sunday? Hope not one of my tuition students.' He moved towards the main door, 'I know your mother would be livid if she saw Prashanti who has this deplorable habit of coming at the wrong time.' He opened the door and to his utter shock and surprise he didn't know how to respond on seeing Dayanand Sharma, his two well-built sons and a few of his henchmen and bouncers.

Without even greeting Rajesh and pushing him gently aside, they entered the living room and glared at Radhika who had a roti in one hand and a piece of chicken in the other. One of the brothers rushed to Radhika, and pulling her by her plait, asked her to wash her hands and return to their house. The car which was outside would take her. Instructing her in the harshest possible manner he said, 'You dare not come to this house again. If we see you here again, we will finish you and this boy. Just go!' He virtually pushed her out of the house.

Dayanand looked at both Manju and Rajesh and said in a loud, assertive and a nasty tone, 'I don't know your exact *jati* (caste) Mr Shankar. You could be a *dom* (untouchable or low caste) or a *chamar* (untouchable or low caste). All Dalits are untouchables and we upper-caste Brahmins have nothing to do with them. We have a separate door in our house from which they enter our bathrooms, clean our shit and leave. You do understand the caste system in this country I hope. We have not made it. It has been made by God and it is due to good karmas in the past life that we have been born in the Brahmin caste. This karma of yours will not release you from the Dalit bondage. Stop messing with my daughter, otherwise you will find this boy's body chopped in a hundred pieces. This is a warning. After this we will not warn you but do what I have just said.' Dayanand left the house with his cronies and his horrible progeny.

Manju sank into the chair and sobbed uncontrollably and Rajesh asked Gaurav to be with Garima. Gaurav didn't meet Radhika during the remaining days of his holidays. His parents implored him to be sensible and sever all contact with Radhika for the time being. Garima was badly shaken up. One night, lying beside Manju she asked her, 'Ma, do you believe in this caste system? What does it actually mean? I think it is very illogical. How can God decide caste and what did that man mean when he said our past karmas determine where we are born? Who keeps the records anyway and what are the criteria for assessing good and bad karmas? What was he talking about?' Manju said, stroking her hair gently, 'Don't worry about all this. You are a beautiful girl and our beloved daughter. This is all that matters. Go to sleep.'

Gaurav returned to the medical college and Garima was busy with her examinations. Manju was also busy in school. Once she saw Radhika in the market and made no attempt to meet her. Radhika, Manju thought, would know how her father and brothers behaved with her and Rajesh. She decided to avoid her and didn't mention it to Rajesh. She noticed that Rajesh had become unusually quiet and quite frail too. One day Rajesh, after breakfast complained of spells of dizziness and Manju insisted that he see a doctor on the same day. He had very high blood pressure and also very high sugar. Manju knew that old age was catching up fast with Rajesh and she had to be mentally prepared and strong enough to look after him and give him the much-needed physical and mental support. She had heard that sometimes, when a person approaches his 80th year, there is a sharp decline in health which also shakes up one's confidence and the will to live and fight it out. She could sense a similar thing happening to Rajesh. She had to be strong and lead the children to their professional success and achievement.

Gaurav had distanced himself from Radhika. He was extremely hurt by what her father told his parents. Gaurav had immense respect for his parents and couldn't understand the caste-based conflict and hatred. He decided to keep away so that his parents had no cause to worry and experience any tension and anxiety. Having witnessed the adverse effects of anxiety on his mother's health he was now aware of his father's ill health too, and he knew that at his age it was dangerous and not a good sign at all. Garima appreciated her brother's attitude and remarked, 'Ma I must say, *bhai* is showing great maturity. We are lucky to have him as the son of the house. I am sure he'll make a name for himself one day.'

Gaurav and Garima did very well professionally. Gaurav completed his MBBS and was on his way to completing his specialisation in neurosurgery. He was very well thought of in the medical fraternity in AFMC .He had showed signs of attaining great heights as a neurosurgeon and was planning to go overseas for super-specialisation. Garima had cleared the IAS exam and after her training she was fortunate to get the Uttar Pradesh cadre which meant that throughout her service, she would be in the state for a large part of her working life. She was happy as this would keep her close to her parents and was especially happy to be near her father as he was getting old. Gaurav and Radhika were not in touch with each other for about seven years. He had not bothered to even find out where she was and how she was doing. She also had made no attempt to meet Gaurav or even write to him. The relationship had broken and Gaurav decided to focus on his career and not get involved in a relationship again.

Manju and Rajesh found themselves lost and empty after the children left home to pursue their respective careers. Manju realised that most of the cooking was done to cater to the taste and the happiness of children. With them not there, there was hardly any work left in the house. Manju missed Garima a lot because she had become her friend and confidante and gave extremely balanced and sensible advice. With advancing age, Manju caught herself becoming uncannily intuitive. Nanno *masi* was on her mind for a few days and she had a feeling that she would be meeting her soon. She also conveyed this to Rajesh. 'I have been thinking of Nanno *masi* recently. I hope all is well with her. It's very strange that I should suddenly think about her after so many days.'

After returning from school one day, she had entered the kitchen to begin preparing dinner when the bell rang. She went to the door, wondering who could come in the evening, and as she opened the door she heard a very familiar voice. It was none other than Nanno *masi*. She was dumbstruck. How could this happen? How and why does a person become intuitive? Is it because of advancing age and the cumulative experiences and knowledge which has a silent impact on the subconscious mind?

Nanno *masi* had grown frail and old. She had come alone and on seeing Manju, broke down and almost collapsed in her arms. She was meeting Manju after seven or eight years and the last time they met was when Manju had visited the Sharma mansion after the demise of Dandi. Nanno *masi* had not been keeping well and had come to Manju knowing that Gaurav had become a doctor and would help in her treatment. Manju said, '*Masi*, Gaurav is still in Pune but we can speak to him on the phone and you can tell him what's wrong. He could tell you what to do or speak to his fellow doctors in the hospital here and we can take you there for a check-up and the treatment.' Nanno *masi* looked relieved and sat down. She asked Manju for a cup of tea. Sipping on the tea she said, 'Manju , I hope your husband does not mind my staying here. You'll have to organise some money for my treatment. I'll repay you later when my chit-fund money comes next month.' Manju assured her that Rajesh would not be angry at all and that money was also not a problem. Both Rajesh and she would be happy to see her get well soon.

Nanno *masi* was diagnosed with an acute anaemic condition, fluctuating blood pressure and advanced osteoporosis. There were no indications of a terminal illness. Gaurav was speaking with her on the telephone on a daily basis and reassured her that she would be perfectly well soon. She was touching 90 and for her age, the going was pretty good. Manju looked after her diet and every day she received Nanno *masi*'s blessings. Rajesh was not particularly fond of her but tolerated her stay and warned Manju not to get involved in any gossip. She was quite a survivor, as wily and crooked as they come. She had spent all her life with the Sharma's in that mansion and Rajesh wondered why she had to come all the way to Manju to be looked after. Surely, the Sharma's should have done this bit for her.

After a week, Nanno *masi* went for another check-up, the results of which indicated good progress. The doctor said that with all her medicines and a prescription for the next month, she could easily travel back. She just needed to be in touch if she ever felt uneasy again. Nanno *masi* told Manju that if it was okay with her and Rajesh, she would like to stay on for another week and then plan her return. Manju had no option except to say that whatever she decided to do was okay with them.

One evening, seeing Manju was free Nanno *masi* walked up to her and taking her permission, sat down for a conversation of sorts. She told Manju that Dayanand met her after his showdown at their place. A year later, Radhika was married into a Brahmin politician's family in Lucknow. Her husband was involved in the family agriculture. For almost two years, Radhika didn't mention the habits of her husband, who turned out to be an alcoholic and a womaniser. Her in-laws were also not good people. The matter flared up when she came in the family way and had big health issues. Her parents brought her back home. It was then that Radhika told them of her miseries. She also had a miscarriage and now she stayed in the Sharma mansion with her parents. The enmity between her husband and her brothers had become intense and had led to many violent encounters. Her husband wanted her back but Dayanand and his sons had put their foot down. One encounter between Radhika's husband and her brothers had led to serious injuries and was almost fatal when one of the brothers sustained a head injury which nearly took his life. He was flown to Lucknow and had a brain operation because of clotting. The boy was still suffering and had fainting spells quite frequently.

Manju heard this detailed story without making a single comment. She didn't want to be entangled in any complication with Radhika or her family. As far as her matter was concerned, it was completely closed for them and Gaurav had moved on. Too much water had flown under the bridge to even take notice of it. However, she was sad to know what had happened with Radhika and her unfortunate marriage. Manju decided to keep Rajesh and the children out of this, and therefore, didn't mention anything to them about Radhika. Nanno *masi* left the following week with a lot of gratitude and good words about how she was looked after by Rajesh and Manju. Both Rajesh and Manju heaved a sigh of relief.

Manju had learnt a number of lessons about leading students in school and leading a number of processes in the institution. However, she was convinced that leading a family was equally challenging, if not more. She learnt that the quality which significantly helped in leading the complexities of the dynamics in a family was discretion. It was absolutely necessary to know when to remain silent and when to speak. Measured speaking was always advantageous. It paid huge dividends later. She had a lot to thank God for. Her children were doing well, she had recovered from her illness and was feeling strong and energetic and Rajesh, for his age, maintained good health. Materially, she had what she needed, and above all, she had a close-knit family with children who stood by her and Rajesh. There was a close bond that they cherished and upheld the family norms and values. The only thing she felt which would give her solid mental peace, was to see both her children married and settled. She was sure that this would also happen in good time.

Gaurav and Garima both came home for Diwali. They were both on a week's holiday. It was a lovely family get-together. Gaurav was also attached to the local hospital as a consultant in the neuro-surgery department and kept coming on work to the hospital once in a while. He was very highly thought of and the hospital had engaged him in the most complicated brain surgery cases lately. Manju, on seeing him getting ready a little early than usual said, 'I hope you are not going to the hospital. You are on Diwali leave and we all expect you to be here, enjoying your leave with us. Please don't get involved in hospital work during this trip. I'll be very disappointed if you vanish for hours from the house.' She patted him on the head and gave him a hug and walked into the kitchen to prepare breakfast for the family. She was joined by Garima and both mother and daughter prepared a sumptuous breakfast, a special Diwali meal.

It was a bracing and a crisp November morning and the family took their cups of tea and sat on a little patch of the well-kept and manicured lawn under a colourful garden umbrella. Gaurav and Garima related hilarious incidents from their work life and Rajesh also had a number of funny tales to share from his days with the bank. As they sat and laughed and chatted away, they saw a caravan of five or six cars turning from the corner of the road approaching their gate. All the cars stood in front of the gate and Dayanand Sharma, his younger son and some other men whom the Shankars didn't recognise, alighted from the cars, walked towards the gate and came in.

Dayanand Sharma greeted Rajesh and Manju with folded hands and stood in front of Rajesh with his head lowered. Both Gaurav and Garima greeted him and asked him to take a chair. Gaurav brought some extra chairs from inside. After a while, with a choked voice and tears welling up in his eyes, Dayanand Sharma spoke in a soft voice to Rajesh and kept his gaze away from Manju. 'My older son is lying in a pool of blood in the hospital. He has sustained fatal head injuries and is unconscious. The doctors in the neuro-surgery department are recommending an immediate operation to stop excessive bleeding. They have stopped us from taking him to Lucknow as they can't guarantee his survival if he is not operated on in the next two hours. Taking him to Lucknow would take more time. They know that your son Gaurav is in town and say that it is only him who can save his life. I have come here to ask him to help us. I need your and his mother's permission and of course his consent. I have no time to say anything else now but would like to speak with you and your family later. Please help me.' Falling on Rajesh's feet, he began to cry and plead to let Gaurav help in the operation.

Rajesh called Manju inside the house. Gaurav served water to all and Garima brought steaming hot cups of tea for the visitors. Rajesh told Manju, 'I know what you feel and how difficult it is to take a decision. There is no time and we have to tell him something.' Manju told him to leave her inside for 10 minutes and asked him to go out and sit with the visitors. She sat on the bed and closed her eyes, beseeching God to guide her and show her the way. Tears rolled down her eyes, tears of anger, disgust, revenge and hatred. The intensity of shame and guilt welled up at the thoughts of being shooed away from the neem tree and warned not to touch it from the old Sharma aunty because she was a Dalit. She had come a long way from there indeed. She got up, settled her saree and walked towards Dayanand Sharma with compassion in her heart and the power and clarity to view the episode from a different and a larger perspective. She stood there like a colossus and said, 'You go with Gaurav now. Garima and I will lock up the house and join you.'

Rajesh looked at her with pride and knew that she was meant for a larger role and would lead in the social and political spheres from Shankargarh shortly. He would live to see her emerge as a strong leader changing the destiny of the Dalits from the district and the state. As these thoughts crossed his mind Manju said, 'My strength comes from you and the support that I received from your mother. This home has given me so much to fall back on in times like this. I have a feeling that this is the beginning of larger work for me. I hope you will be okay with my long spells of absence from home?' She looked expectantly at Rajesh. 'Your growth and your happiness are very important for me. There is nothing else which will give me more pride than your achievements. So just move on and do what you are meant to do.' Saying these words Rajesh moved towards the scooter and waited for Manju and Garima so that he could drop them to the hospital.

Gaurav and the doctors of the local hospital fought a hard battle for a couple of days to save Dayanand Sharma's son's life. He was virtually touch and go, but after three days, despite being in partial coma, his other health indicators had more or less stabilised. It was then decided that he would be airlifted and taken to All India Medical Institute (AIIMS) for brain surgery to remove the blood clots from his brain. Dayanand requested Gaurav to go with the doctor's team to Delhi and stay there till the surgery was performed. Manju and Rajesh agreed and so did Gaurav. His son had lost movement in his left leg and arm and could regain some mobility only after months of physiotherapy. He remained in the hospital for almost four months.

Dayanand Sharma requested Manju to join the ruling party in Uttar Pradesh and also head a government aided organisation for the education and skilling of Dalit boys and girls in remote and backward villages in the state. Manju accepted the offer and worked tirelessly for two years. Her work was appreciated by the party and the ministers and she was offered a ticket to fight the state level elections after two years. She represented the Dalit communities in the state and, with the support of the community, won by a huge lead in the elections. She got to head the Schedule Caste and the Tribal ministries at the state level and was an active member of the Vidhan Sabha.

During her swearing in and oath-taking ceremony Mrs Sharma of the *haveli* where her mother worked, was present. She was very old and frail but congratulated Manju at the good work which she was doing and also invited her for tea with the chief minister. Rajesh advised her to be gracious and accept the invitation. She was accompanied by Gaurav and Garima and there, after years, she met Radhika, Dayanand Sharma's daughter. Radhika, being a widow, wore a white sari and greeted her with affection and respect. Gaurav had moved on and had a friend who was also a doctor in AFMC and was planning to marry her.

Gaurav's marriage was an extremely dignified affair with a number of dignitaries from Delhi and Lucknow. In fact, all the state government ministers and officials were present. Dayanand Sharma walked up to Rajesh and Manju and said, 'I hear that Gaurav and his wife plan to open a nursing home in Shankargarh to serve the local community and also stay close to you and Rajesh so that he can look after you. He has been brought up extremely well and it's a matter of great pride for any parent to have children like yours.' Manju discerned a film of tears in his eyes and thanking them he quietly walked away.

Debunath Moitra—People Lead from Where They Stand

We often mistake speakers and instructors for leaders. The world all over has made the mistake of giving leadership roles to people who are glib talkers, people who can instruct and control. Leading a nation and an organisation is not possible by one individual alone. Organisations and nation states are led by many people working together, in collaboration and coordination. Any innovation and major transformation is a result of collective aspirations and efforts where each and every individual's energy and will is significantly instrumental for achieving the developmental goals. Leadership therefore, is a process which is managed by many people. The dreams and vision of individuals coalesce to form a compelling vision, directing groups and communities towards change and transformation. Unless the vision is owned by people its energy is not sufficiently powerful to ignite, move and sustain a transformational journey. Organisational visions gain credibility when their themes reflect, for every individual, his or her personal vision too. In this way organisational and personal visions are also integrated.

Large scale change and highly effective and sustained levels of performance are a result of strong leadership processes developed, designed, embedded and implemented in organisations. People perform different roles in such processes. I would like to dispel the notion that there is always one leader whose vision and work can bring and sustain great transformation. This is next to impossible. Transformation and development is the result of leadership processes and the relevant and various skills required to manage and sustain them. The story related in the following pages reflects these beliefs and tenets about leadership.

The setting of this story is the district Murshidabad in West Bengal. Located in the east of India, it is known for its art and craft, lush greenery and thick forests. The place is predominantly inhabited by fishing communities who reside in the plains and all along the coastal areas. The Ganga river falls into the Bay of Bengal and as it meanders from the Himalayas across the northern states into Bengal, it boasts of a number of ancient towns and erstwhile kingdoms which sprung up along its fertile shores.

The Murshidabad district is situated on the left bank of the Ganga and Murshidabad city got its name from the district. It is a populous district. All of Bengal was once governed and ruled from here and after the then Nawab, Siraj-Ud-Daula, lost the battle of Plassey to the British, the capital was shifted to Calcutta which is now called Kolkata. Murshidabad is an agricultural and silk-trading centre and emperors like Akbar and Aurangzeb made great efforts to develop this area. For a long time, the British, after winning the battle of Plassey, ruled from here and rendered great power and privileges to the district. The district was named Murshidabad after the Nawab Murshid Quli Khan. Like the other areas of West Bengal, Murshidabad also played a significant role in India's freedom struggle. The Murshidabad District Congress Committee was formed in 1921 and stalwarts of the freedom struggle, from Mahatma Gandhi, to Subhas Chandra Bose, Kazi Nazrul Islam, C.R. Das, Dr. Rajendra Prasad had all visited Murshidabad during the freedom struggle.

The Bhagirathi and the Jalangi rivers flow through this illustrious district. Most of the arable land is used for agricultural purposes and the lush alluvial soil is well-suited for the growth of neem, mango and jackfruit trees.

The story is set in this geographical context and the historical and the socio-political background of Murshidabad district. The story unfolded in Raghunathpur, a village on the left bank of the river Bhagirathi, about 50 kilometres from the city. The story begins in the late forties and the early fifties. The biggest zamindar in Raghunathpur was Sirji Debunath Moitra. He was a Brahmin. He belonged to a pious and cultured family of erudite pandits who had earned the respect of the local community, including the Muslims who outnumbered the Hindus, not only in Raghunathpur but in the entire Murshidabad district itself.

Debunath Moitra was called Sirji in the village; he had obtained three post-graduate degrees. These degrees were in English literature, political science and history. He believed that all human beings had a right to be educated and those who were poor and couldn't afford education needed to be supported by the government and the rich gentry. Education would not only change the destiny of individuals but also positively impact societal and cultural processes in communities and societies.

Unfortunately there were no schools in the village, and those who had money and were keen on educating their children in boarding schools in Kolkata.

The poor, in any case, couldn't afford any form of education. Sirji had discussed this issue many times with the panchayat members who appreciated his thoughts and concerns. Sirji had told them, 'I could personally organise it in a small way in the beginning, but then it would require a team of hard-working and committed people to take the project forward. I am planning to collect at least 10 willing children and teach them the basics of Bengali and English and gradually expose them to simple arithmetic. If I persist in my efforts and the children show interest, and if they get support from their families, then we can do something in the area. This will be like a small pilot project. I know that it will be very difficult to bring the girls to the classes but I will definitely try to do this'.

Sirji requested the panchayat members to make a plan on how this message should be spread amidst the village community, trusting them to strategise in the best possible way so that their intentions were not misunderstood and the families supported and collaborated in this small project. The panchayat was by and large supportive except for a few members who thought that this would be a waste of money and effort. Where, they thought, would this little bit of education lead the children? After all, they'd have to work on the farms or as labourers and the girls would be married off in their teens, do household chores, look after the cows and buffaloes in their houses and give birth to children. This was the fate of the poor generally in these areas.

Sirji ignored the dissent of the few members and encouraged the others to contact the families. To his surprise, within a week, he received feedback from 35 families that they were keen on sending their children and most said that their daughters would also attend. The only reassurance they wanted was about the safety and security of the girls. All together, the children were totalling to 69. Sirji was quite excited by the response and decided to formalise the pilot project and launch the classes in a month's time.

Prakash and Arun, two members of the panchayat, did a lot of the running around to organise the classes. Sirji allotted four rooms attached to the outer courtyard of his *haveli* and provided money for the lights and a few pieces of furniture. A large number of tables and chairs were also taken from the warehouse of the *haveli* and repaired and polished. All other material for classes, such as pens, notebooks, pencils and maps were purchased from the local market. The panchayat members found the work different and engaging and were happy at the response of the community.

Prakash and Arun invited a few decent and educated local politicians and traders from the *tehsil* towns in the neighbourhood as well as a few village elders. The families of all the students were also invited. Some parents of the students volunteered to organise snacks for the inauguration and also set up a makeshift stage for the leaders to sit on and address the students. Prakash and Arun wrote the welcome speeches for Sirji and a few parents. The inauguration commenced on time and the school was launched on 15 August 1951 in Raghunathpur. This was the first school in the village and the leaders envisioned it to be a harbinger of change and progress, not only in Raghunathpur, but in Murshidabad district itself. Sirji, in his late thirties, a couple of years away from his 40th year planted the first seed of formal education, hoping that the others would also lead and nurture the school and consistently and actively build it brick by brick.

Students, both boys and girls from all castes, religious groups and socio-economic classes, were admitted in the school. It was called the Raghunathpur Primary School and began with basic literacy and numeracy classes. The group of 69 students were divided into four sections. Age was not considered a criterion of admission. The leadership, comprising of Sirji, Arun, Prakash and fathers of five children, took a decision that as it was extremely difficult to determine the exact age of the children in a village in India—at a time when parents didn't keep a record of birth dates and years—it was best to ignore this criterion as there would not be any examination to clear and promotions to higher classes during the first year. The first year was a period of experimentation and assessment of the interest, talent and motivation in students for studying further. In this year, their experience of teaching, how teaching methods and styles were received by the students, what worked well and what didn't, would help in understanding how academic processes, activities and administrative operations could be planned and implemented better.

The major day-to-day workload was borne by Prakash and Arun and the other five volunteers who also pitched in substantially, taking time out from their farming activities and other routines.

Attendance was regular and the students were picking up fast. Sirji suspected that a few girls were also in their early twenties. Teaching was carried out in Bengali and Sirji decided that he would not burden the students with additional inputs in arithmetic for another three months at least. Homework was also not given to the students as most of them had to share the responsibility of household work and the boys had to help in the farming activities after school. Some also supplemented the family income by working as daily-wage labourers.

There were some hiccups in the first three months regarding attendance of girls, especially during any puja which was celebrated in the village. They helped their mothers and aunts in the preparations. Education for them, in any case, was not at all a priority and it was surprising that the families allowed the girls to attend classes in the first place. Just casually, Arun mentioned to Sirji one evening, 'I am a little worried watching a few boys becoming familiar with the girl students. We must ask them to be careful. This is Murshidabad, a predominantly Muslim area, and you would appreciate Sirji, that if anything were to happen to a girl in school, and that too between a Hindu and a Muslim, we would witness a bloody massacre, not only in Raghunathpur but in all of Murshidabad district. This could well lead to immense communal tension in the entire state. We have to be vigilant and careful about this. I sometimes wonder how the parents from Muslim families permitted their girls to attend these classes. Prakash and I were discussing this with the panchayat members, who you know represent the thought process of the community, and they mentioned that it is largely because of your credibility, character and respect that this could happen. They also look upon you as a saintly man who has not even married and raised his own family. They marvel at your discipline and detachment from worldly matters and look up to you because of your education, wisdom and balance.'

Debunath Moitra heard Arun praise him with humility and gratitude. For the first time, he understood what his image and reputation was in the community. He was the only child of Raghubir Moitra and Prabha Devi. His father was also an only child of his parents. His forefathers had served the British and thus acquired land and wealth which the British had given them for their loyalty and services. Raghubir Moitra was very fair with light blue eyes and could easily be mistaken for an Englishman. He spoke impeccable English. At the age of 18, Raghubir Moitra discovered that his mother was raped by an Englishman and the matter was hushed up when his father accepted a huge bounty by the British. Raghubir Moitra had deep hatred for his father and pitied his mother, who passed away when he was 12 years old.

Prabha Devi was the eldest daughter of Maulana Asif Ali from the Murshidabad city. Raghubir met her at a common friend's place in Murshidabad during his visits to settle accounts of his father's business which traded in jute. She belonged to the backward caste settled along the coast of what is now Bangladesh. It was largely a Muslim fishing community, generally uneducated and poor. Her original name was changed from Parveen Ali to Prabha Devi. So Debunath Moitra was a half Hindu, upper-caste Brahmin and half Muslim. No Brahmin family was prepared to marry his daughter to him. Debunath had inherited a slight burgundy tint in his hair from his father. His mother had typical Bengali looks, with a dark complexion and curly, thick black hair. Everyone believed that his fair colour and hair were because of his being a high-caste Brahmin. Raghubir Moitra joined the Quit India Movement and died in jail fighting the British. Prabha Devi couldn't take the shock and passed away soon thereafter, leaving Debunath orphaned while he was in his late teens. Debunath's life history was quite complicated and therefore he grew up as a complicated child. He was not particularly close to his parents and after his mother's demise became a recluse, surrounded himself with books and looked after the upkeep and the maintenance of his *haveli*. In his teens, he ran into big property and huge family wealth. However, managing it was a nightmare and he often thought that boys of his age who didn't have this burden to carry and had freedom and space to invest time in their hobbies and pursuits of interest were very fortunate. This feeling gradually grew into a dislike for too much money and properties that needed to be looked after.

Even in his teens, Debunath began to perceive the subtle power plays in the *haveli* amongst those staff members who had anything to do with his money and property management directly or indirectly. These experiences as a teenager made him realise the importance of education in the broadest sense possible, not only through post-graduate degrees but also expanding his repertoire of reading which included philosophy, astronomy, astrology and many other academic disciplines. He was an avid reader of T.S. Eliot as well P.G. Wodhouse, biographies of almost anyone who had contributed to the development of thought and civilisation, including great political leaders and social reformists. By the time he reached 35, his personal library had a collection of over 5,000 books which boasted of a wide and versatile collection.

The loneliness in his growing years and the lack of company of siblings or friends—most families in Raghunathpur kept away from the *haveli* in awe, respect or fear—made Debunath develop the tendency to introspect and reflect. There was a continuous churning in his heart and a silent search for an identity and purpose to live. His mixed up caste and religious lineage didn't make this simple. Even though his surname proclaimed his membership in the *kuleen* (high-caste) Brahmin family, he hardly understood the meaning of this membership and how much it contributed to making him who he was. What was it to behave like a Brahmin in West Bengal and in India? He didn't have these behavioural examples available in the house which could make him identify and internalise the upper-caste ethos of the zamindari.

The search for personal identity and roots can be both painful and exciting. The pain lies in the confusion and the regret of experiencing an inadequacy of not knowing the language, the traditions and the people of the community or the nation where the moorings of identity need to be found and strengthened. One yearns to belong but knows that many things are required to be achieved before acceptance and comfort are possible. The connection with people is very important and after all, we ultimately must belong to someone and to many others through the network of relationships in our lives. A reciprocal relationship is the vehicle through which roots and identities are built and strengthened. Debunath's biggest problem lay in his aversion for social interaction of any kind.

Perhaps this was because of the fear of letting people know the background of his mother and his grandmother. He was afraid of prying questions and the gossip that might ensue once the information about his family was disclosed to others. Debunath felt that once people came close enough, they began to ask personal questions out of sheer curiosity or malice. No one could stop the irresponsible gossip and loose talk that followed. He was thankful to God for giving him the sense which made him keep far from gossip and politics. Life was peaceful and uncomplicated. But, there was this yearning to belong and more closely identify with the community. He didn't know his people at all. Arun was right in reminding him about the problems that would take place if a Muslim boy and Hindu girl were to get into a relationship. He had not thought about this as it was inconsequential for him. However, it appeared that this was the reality that needed to be accepted, understood and managed. Had he made a mistake by opening a school with so much caste, class, communal and cultural diversity? Even the age of students could lead to problems. This would require a high level of sensitivity, perceptiveness, maturity and perhaps transformational leadership competencies to handle. The vision of unity in diversity had to be understood, internalised and lived by each and every student and staff member. With these thoughts, Debunath called it a day and prepared to go to sleep.

Winter was fast approaching and there was already a nip in the air. The *haveli* rooms had very high ceiling which made them cold and gloomy. They were like mini halls and each room could easily accommodate 150–200 people. The school only had 15 students in each section and as the number was so small, hardly one-fourth of the classroom space was occupied. Arun and Prakash felt that the numbers of students could be increased from January and a small token amount could be charged from each student which would gradually help in building a corpus for the school. They also believed that anything free was not valued. They requested for a meeting with Debunath who suggested that parents and panchayat members should also be called to the meeting as these were sensitive issues to be tabled. Obtaining everybody's views would give them confidence to take decisions and also enrol the community in later implementation. Prakash felt that a few mature male and female students should also be invited to the meeting.

The meeting ended in a few important decisions. Student strength would only increase once proper classes started. In the first year, the teaching was completely unstructured and no prescribed books were used by the teachers or the students. It was unorganised teaching only to impart numeracy and literacy to a mixed group. Also, proper fees would be charged once structured classes commenced. It was pointless asking children to pay even a nominal token amount presently. The composition of students would remain the same and boys and girls would not be segregated into separate classes. If this worked without any major problems that year, then it could continue afterwards too.

Things in the school were working out well. Attendance had stabilised at 97 per cent. All the teachers were dedicated and put in great effort in making every student learn at the highest level of his or her capability. The students were highly motivated. The girls were slightly ahead in their performances as compared to the boys. Parents kept visiting the schools and very sweetly kept bringing small gifts like flower vases, mats to sit on, wall hangings and some even volunteered in the upkeep of the garden. Time flew and the school had already completed eight months of smooth running. A group of journalists visited the school one morning and wanted to meet Debunath. They had heard praises about this small effort by the community and wanted to cover the story in a Bengali and an English newspaper. Debunath initially was hesitant to talk about the school with anyone but after being persuaded by his senior team of teachers, community members and parents of students, he agreed to have a meeting. After a few weeks, there were beautiful articles on the classes. The effort of everyone who was involved was appreciated in the article and there was a lot of praise for Debunath. A number of inquiries about the classes as well as the plan for the school started coming to Debunath, Arun and Prakash. They suddenly came into a lot of limelight.

The attendance in the classes was stable, the students were progressing well and those who were involved in teaching were also putting in their best. Above all, there was a positive and a cheerful atmosphere in the school. Nine months had passed and there were no unpleasant incidents. The apprehension about managing diversity, especially the presence of boys and girls together, had not posed a problem at all. There was a lot of cohesion amongst students and Debunath, on many occasions, saw them even sharing food. These were good signs of social change and Debunath felt that if things continued like this, he could easily persuade the government authorities to give the school the formal status of a primary school with a number of facilities and schemes for the students. This could help the students in obtaining scholarships, a mid-day meal facility and a lot of other subsidies, once the school was declared as an institution set up for the poorest of the poor.

Debunath had a faint sense of achievement for the first time in his life. Feeling happy and light-hearted, he said to Jamuna, his maid, 'Why don't you prepare some good food for lunch today? I'll also ask Arun and Prakash to join me. Today I won't invite their families. I'll organise a bigger lunch some other time. They can bring their families then. Make some two three different types of fish, some mutton, dal and vegetables.

'I leave the sweet dish decision to you. Ask Sarju to do the shopping. You have enough people to help you in the kitchen'.

Arun and Prakash came on time and brought packets of beautiful *agarbattis* for the puja *ghar*. Debunath was touched by their thoughtfulness.

For the first time Debunath felt at home in his own *haveli*. He had not shared a meal with anyone for years. Even as a child, he never ate with his parents. His father ate separately and his mother ate after finishing all the work and supervision for the day. He was served in a small silver thali in the veranda on his tiny dining table and his father told him, 'You sit here and eat. I ate on this table as a little child. My father was very strict about meal timings and didn't appreciate if children fussed about food. So you eat what is given to you. Many children go without food. Consider yourself lucky. But luck doesn't last forever...do you understand? No fuss.' Arun and Prakash looked at each other and understood his loneliness as a child. They also understood that he had grown up to be a lonely man, suppressed and sad. Debunath enjoyed the evening and after the two left, he thought that he would organise many such evenings in the future. Company made such a difference to everything, to life itself. He looked at the mirror and thought that he still appeared young and healthy, in fact, he thought he was quite good-looking. He decided to dress better and be well groomed. It would make a difference to his image.

From that evening onwards, Debunath began to socialise and discovered the happiness and satisfaction that friends and even acquaintances could bring. He became interested in clothes and perfumes and even in the upkeep and the beautification of the *haveli*. People also saw a different Debunath and many commented that he was a good-looking man with a pleasing personality who had rather winsome ways with the ladies. He developed quite a fan following of ladies in Raghunathpur. There was a new life in the *haveli* and the staff appeared to be more energetic as they had something to do in the weekends for which they prepared during the week, like cleaning, polishing, purchasing grocery and organising the crockery and the cutlery.

Debunath's life appeared to be transforming. He was involved in work and his social life became active and satisfying. He was taking interest in himself and in the decoration and the maintenance of the *haveli*. He realised that both were time-consuming tasks but he was enjoying them equally. Many people commented that he looked younger and more energetic. This boosted his self-confidence. His visits to the school increased and he was getting to know the students personally, but he always maintained a discrete distance with the female students. He was continually aware of the conversation that he had had with Arun in the past. In the given situation, he realised, discretion was better than valour. He couldn't afford to risk his reputation at all and hated the idea of too much familiarity with people because of their tendency to pry into private and personal matters. However Debunath was not in the habit of taking decisions that had a far-reaching impact on people, processes and outcomes. He therefore, dilly-dallied making decisions and his consistency and focus on critical points would waver as his thoughts would become confused.

Even though he understood that it was wise to stay away from the students, there were moments when he felt that there was nothing wrong in becoming friendly with them, including the girls. At his age and status, no one would object to his interaction with students, and in any case for all the girls in school, he was more like a father figure.

One evening while Debunath was walking back from the *haveli*, Asma, a Muslim student, followed him and before he entered the gate she called out to him. 'Sir, sir, please stop. I want to speak with you about an important matter.' Debunath turned back and saw her standing behind him. He asked, 'What is the matter?' Asma said, 'Sir, I want to discuss something personal with you. It has been bothering me for a number of days.'

Debunath was standing outside his *haveli* gate and thought that it wouldn't be wise to continue standing and talking to her there. 'Come in, please follow me.' He took Asma inside and sat with her in the outer sitting room where normally he met the people of the village and conducted meetings with government officials. It was a well-appointed room, elegant and very functional. The staff saw him and came in and asked whether he would like tea and snacks. 'Yes, yes, why don't you get some tea and something to eat.'

He looked at Asma and asked her to tell him what the matter was. Asma was a pretty girl in her late twenties. She belonged to a poor family of weavers and also knew weaving. She helped her family in the trade. Asma had always wanted to study but the family lacked the financial resources to educate her. After a long wait, she found Debunath's school which didn't charge fees and as a result, even though reluctantly, her parents and other elders in the family allowed her to attend the classes. 'But a few days ago sir, I heard that the school will be charging fees. I can't afford to pay and hence I will have to leave the school when that happens. This has been disturbing me a lot.' Debunath didn't know how to respond, so hurriedly and unsurely, he said, 'Oh, there is nothing to worry about. This was the idea, but we could definitely find a solution for it. I'll speak to the school administration and see how we can help students like you. There is nothing to worry about. You continue coming to class '.

Arun appeared to be agitated when he met Debunath the next day in school and he said, 'Sirji, it is better that you don't interact with students. You told Asma something about the fees not being charged by the school and now this has spread among the group of students. They now think that we won't be charging fees at all, even in the future. This is ridiculous. How can a student meet you at home? You entertain her, give her tea and snacks and then tell her that she needn't worry about fees at all. Can we ever establish this school? Do you have any idea about the amount of money which is required to run a school decently? Moreover you should not be speaking to Muslim girls so freely and that too at the *haveli* in the evening.'

Arun didn't let Debunath say a word and before leaving in a huff he mentioned that, 'Prakash and I are working very hard at the school. We don't take a penny. Please understand that we require resources to manage our families. We arc not as lucky as you are, with no responsibility and all the money and luxury in the world. We also work elsewhere to make both ends meet. Once the school begins to earn from fees, we too can get our salaries which will be of immense help.' Arun had left Debunath completely bewildered and dumbstruck. He felt small and foolish. He had not given this aspect any thought. Arun was correct about the money which Prakash and he needed to run their families. However, he was convinced that Arun was making a mountain out of a molehill by giving too much importance to his meeting with Asma. A little socialising with the students would bring no harm. Debunath decided to be careful and not attract undue attention. Building and leading a school was not everybody's cup of tea and with these thoughts, Debunath decided to retire to the *haveli* early.

Asma had not shared the truth with Debunath. She was twice divorced and had a four-year-old son from her first marriage. She had been turned out of the house by her second husband, who was sure that she was meeting another man in the village. Her parents had refused to provide any kind of shelter for her. She had gone wayward and greedy. She was very fond of the good life, stylish clothes, jewellery, make-up and good food. The *haveli*, its opulence and grandeur, attracted her and she was jealous of the rich whom, she thought, had it all in life and were treated partially by God and destiny. She kept remembering the carpets, chandeliers and the decorative pieces at the *haveli* when Debunath had called her in for that small conversation. How she wished she had been able to spend more time there! The snacks, the cutlery and crockery were incredibly beautiful and for the first time, she understood that royalty and the rich were particular about everything that they needed in the house.

That night she thought that she would have been lucky if Debunath had a son like him. He would surely be attracted to her. She was quite good-looking, had the classic features and the colour of her Pathan lineage, and her mother apart, from being fair had brown hair and grey green eyes.

That whole week in school, Asma kept looking for Debunath and on some pretext or the other made attempts to strike a conversation with him. Whenever she saw him, she tried guessing his age and then came to a conclusion that he would be between 45–50, only 18 or at the most, 20 years older than her. That night as she tried hard to sleep, she kept thinking about Debunath and the *haveli*. Innumerable thoughts raced through her mind as she closed her eyes and concluded that many women also marry much older men. She thought that almost all the time, such marriages worked out because after a while, as the husband grew older, he got out of the way of the wife and was preoccupied with his failing health, security and financial responsibilities and left the wife on her own. This worked out for the wife because she obtained her freedom, retained her mobility and youth and could indulge in many other interests, including a few illicit relationships if need be. She had learnt the lessons that her life had taught her and was very much a woman of the world.

Prakash, the second panchayat member who actively helped in the school with Arun and Debunath, had witnessed the fleeting interactions between Asma and Debunath and had also noticed that the interactions were increasing. Others in the school, he was sure, must have noticed it too. This worried him a bit as he knew a little about Asma's background and instinctively didn't like her. Prakash was a clean and straightforward man who could manage his boundaries very well. He met Arun one evening and said, 'You know Arun, Debunath and his meetings with that student, Asma, are worrying me. He doesn't seem to realise that very soon this will go out of the *haveli* and stir a hornet's nest and get us into a lot of trouble. What has come over this Debunath? I haven't heard very good things about Asma.'

'I've discussed this with Debunath and obviously he has not given this too much importance. Times have changed and no one bothers about zamindars and their zamindaris. Debunath feels that no one in Raghunathpur can lift a finger against him. He doesn't know that today they can brutally kill him and ransack his *haveli* and finish off everything. You are right, the girl has had two marriages before and has a little son. Her parents don't entertain her in their home. I believe that she is living with an aunt nearby. For establishing an institution, the leaders have to be cognizant of what is going on outside in the community and the environment. Debunath lives in his own world. I don't know what to do about this.'

Prakash decided to meet Debunath at the *haveli* in the evening. When he approached the *haveli,* he saw a number of rooms which were normally not used by Debunath, lit up and their windows open. He thought that maybe he had some people over in the evening. When he reached the gate he saw his study also well-lit and even the corridors and the living rooms were lighted. He asked the guard at the main gate if there was a big party taking place inside. 'No sir, there is no party. Sirji is in the haveli.' Prakash entered the lobby area in front and to his shock and amazement he saw Debunath holding Asma's hand and walking with her. He was explaining the structure of the *haveli*, the architectural details and other things. He stood for almost five to seven minutes in one place without moving or uttering a single word and saw what was happening. Asma had umpteen questions to ask and was very curious about the *haveli*, about Debunath's family and his existing and active family relationships. Prakash thought that apart from being extremely foolish, Debunath didn't realise the extreme sensitivity and complication of the situation. If he continued behaving the way he was, the whole Muslim community in Murshidabad district would be up in arms. After all, he was not a young man. He was a middle-aged man expected to display more maturity and foresight.

Debunath saw Prakash, looked embarrassed and tried explaining Asma's interest in the history of the *haveli* and her natural curiosity and intelligence to ask pertinent questions. Prakash thought that she was more interested in the future and personal plans of Debunath rather than any historical facts about the *haveli*. Asma's questions were a clever and roundabout way of assessing the wealth of the *haveli* and its owner. How could Debunath not understand it?

After Asma left, Prakash sat with Debunath in the study and opening the conversation said, 'For both

Arun and me, obtaining financial support from the school on a monthly basis in the form of salaries after April would be crucial. We have to look after our families and have many other responsibilities. Establishing an institution which is financially viable is not a child's play. It requires dedication, hard work and a lot of planning and also leading the community and the people within. I hope you realise this, Debunath. Arun and I have already put in about six months of work without being compensated at all. However, we can't carry on like this. We three also have to be very clear about our vision for the school and our specific roles. Why don't we meet sometime this week? In fact, the sooner it's done the better, so that we could discuss and begin to set our goals and targets and make a plan for the next year at least.'

Debunath was shocked by what he heard. All this while he thought that it was his idea, he was the leader and owner and had sufficient political clout in Raghunathpur and Murshidabad to enrol the panchayat and the district administration in his hobbies and interests. He was the zamindar and the others would naturally follow without any doubts or questions. What was Prakash talking about, what common vision for the school did he have in mind?

It was only his vision which was important. Yes, he had to articulate it soon so that the team was aware and could make suitable plans to commence the work. Arun and Prakash, he thought, were also becoming too big for their boots. They had no business interfering in his personal affairs and give him lectures on Asma and his behaviour with her.

Debunath didn't understand the difference between leading through positional power and control and leading through a vision and partnership. Arun and Prakash believed that leading the community was complex and establishing an institution in Raghunathpur required a completely different mindset and approach. They felt helpless and came to the conclusion that it would be difficult to carry on working with Debunath on the project. They had begun to understand the feudal mindset of Debunath and the arrogance that he had about his money and power.

Wars are fought in the mind first, everything must emanate from the heart and mind. Mental and emotional processes must transform first before being translated into transformational skills, work and achievement. Therefore, the mind must think differently and the heart must feel differently in order that new and different goals are achieved. This is easier said than done. Rigid and structured mindsets cannot lead innovative and transformational work. Most leadership work is in innovation, change, transformation and breakthrough performance and achievement. Positional power and arrogance of money and control comes in the way of transformation and building an institution rather than being facilitative. It is, therefore, not easy to manage the complexity of positional power and the demands of teamwork, humility and openness to learn and support failure during journeys of transformation and change. The first requirement is to manage the self and if need be bring about a lot of self-level change. This is not everyone's cup of tea.

Leaders who lead change and innovate, those who are entrepreneurs and transform old and feudal systems and thinking, stay in touch with the community and are connected with their aspirations. This makes it possible to understand how the community, or for that matter, if we juxtapose this narrative for organisations, even the employees, are envisioning their future. They are able to relate to and articulate the dreams of the people they lead. Leadership is not only about leading people individually and collectively. Leaders are also the part of the public they lead. So they are responsible for leading themselves too. There are a number of people who distinctly perform the leadership role all times in society and organisations. Therefore, it is imperative to dispel the notion that there is only one leader who leads the transformation process. In fact for one singular person this is too big and impossible a task to do. It is seen that leaders who understand and lead themselves well are those who successfully lead others. The reverse is not possible and is not true.

Debunath had not understood this at all despite his wide reading. He lacked exposure and had never interacted with the community. He led a very secluded and insular life and had no clue about the changes that were gradually but surely coming in to Raghunathpur. The younger generation was moving towards self-reliance and independence and aspiring for freedom in speech, life choices and the courage to assert their will and their rights. In some ways, they looked down upon the concept of zamindari and the zamindars with disdain.

Building a school which would encourage diversity and gender equality was an innovative and transformational idea. However its implementation needed to be carried out with a lot of sensitivity and maturity and also required to be managed in a quiet and subtle manner. Debunath's behaviour was far from this. He had thrown all caution to the wind and his behaviour with Asma was not only objectionable but also undermined his leadership stature and respect.

Debunath's visits to the school were becoming infrequent. However the frequency of Asma's visits to the *haveli* was increasing. Noticing this, both Arun and Prakash decided to take about a month to figure out whether they would like to continue their association with Debunath and his school or not. They didn't see a possibility of the school being established well in the future without a vision or commitment. Debunath would expect them to keep running the classes and would not be able to dedicate his time to build anything larger and more purposeful. He certainly wouldn't be interested in earning from the school, and therefore, Arun and Prakash wouldn't obtain any financial support from the school which they needed.

A week later, Arun and Prakash met Debunath and told him that they would like to dissociate from the school and spend their time elsewhere. Debunath looked a little shocked and disturbed. They left the school after a month and handed over the papers to Debunath. In that meeting, Debunath mentioned that he had planned to give them accommodation in the *haveli* and would have been keen on letting them shift in with their families. After a while, once they had settled in, all the facilities of the haveli would have been extended to them. They would have led a comfortable life and their children would have inherited huge property.

Arun and Prakash thanked him and told him, 'We are not zamindars. We like to work hard for our living and work honestly. Educating our children is our first priority. We are good where we are and surely in the months and years to come we would be able to do something with our careers and life.'

Arun and Prakash resumed their work with the Raghunathpur panchayat with more rigour. A rich farmer was keen to offer his three-acre plot for building a school for boys and girls and he was also keen on spending money in setting up the infrastructure. They took up this challenge happily and were successful in bringing together a competent and an enthusiastic team. However, the greatest challenge initially was not in learning how to establish a new institution but in unlearning and undoing a number of things that had been done in the past. Leading the processes of unlearning and undoing are significantly important for leaders, as through such effort, they remove the stubborn blocks in the path of achieving major goals and meaningful purpose.

The Need for Achievement

In his classic treatise on human motivation, David McClleland distinguished between the need for power, affiliation, achievement and avoidance. The need for achievement is associated with motivation derived from the attainment of difficult targets and goals, taking calculated and moderate risks, competitiveness and the satisfaction from solving problems, innovation and creativity. All these human motives are learnt during socialisation in particular cultures and traditions and interplay with more complex human constructs like personality, approaches to learning and the various mechanisms of behavioural reinforcement.

Economic progress and industrialisation with technological breakthroughs are good examples of the need for achievement and working towards setting best practices and benchmarks. The need for achievement creates propensities to compete with oneself by attempts to continuously increase the learning curve and raising the personal bars of performance standards. However even though this need is learnt through culture specific processes, it is gradually internalised and sinks deep below the waterline into the subconscious to influence personal and professional choices, the attitudes towards timelines, challenging targets and the excitement and exhilaration in beating standards and metrics of past achievements. An obvious corollary of the need for achievement is the motivation to compete, not necessarily always with others but definitely with oneself. Consequently the ambition and the drive for success are also strong.

Effective leaders are more focussed on the fulfilment of team goals and are driven to realise organisational visions rather than personal goals and ambitions. For doing so they enlist members of the team in the journey to success and breakthrough performances and ensure that the voice of the team is listened to. In this way, the energy and the motivation of the team is maintained. The task and people orientation are both high when leaders are propelled by a high need to achieve as nothing worthwhile can be achieved, and later sustained, if the team is not together and willing. The long term vision and purpose instils pride in the team, which helps them go beyond monetary and positional reinforcements and anchor work engagement in the big picture. The need for achievement also generates sustained action and attainment of results and implementation, execution of plans and a sense of completion and closure. There is a lot of visible action and evolving perfection in action and continuous learning. Emphasis is on proactive behaviour, taking initiative and risk, experimentation and solving problems and generating novel ideas and solutions on the way.

Ambition is not a negative syndrome. It is certainly not the opposite of contentment. Ambition is the desire to do something and not always for personal success, wealth or fame and even if it is and the person shares it with others and gives others a fair opportunity for meaningful work and success it is a good thing. Ambition is bad when it becomes exploitative. Bill and Melinda Gates couldn't spend billions on health care round the world if they weren't ambitious enough to create such wealth and obviously they have created huge personal wealth too. David McClleland studied the achievement motive and discovered that it is learnt from childhood and is culture specific. He analysed hundreds of stories that mothers told their growing children and found that achieving societies have mothers who relate stories of ambition, achievement and success to their growing toddlers and children. These stories are gradually internalised and even personal, familial, organisational and national success themes impact subconsciously and all these themes are connected and integrated for creating motivation and drives. McClleland has represented his seminal research in his book *The Achieving Society*.

Leaders and leadership processes facilitate personal achievement and achievement of teams and organisations. Corporate, organisational and national leadership processes display the presence of achievement motivation. In today's world, a healthy competitiveness, the drive to attain goals and targets and the ambition for success is necessary to excel, grow and even survive. The bars and benchmarks of success are being continuously raised. We cannot become negatively complacent and contented on the performance-front at all.

There are many areas of achievement. For leaders the focus of achievement worldwide is shifting from mere economic and financial goals to many others, even in the corporate organisations. Leaders and leadership processes are successful if through them other leaders are developed and the leadership bench strength is buttressed. This can only be achieved when leaders invest their time in understanding talent and potential, and organise for their growth and learning through financial resources, delegation and enriching roles and enlarging responsibilities.

Coaching has become a significantly important domain for leading people. Leaders have a sense of achievement by providing learning support to young people and establishing a trusting relationship with them. This is a perceptible shift from personal and positional power orientation to ensuring the success of team members and also the entire team. The belief in tough love is gaining importance and trust and support is seen to emanate from it. At any hierarchical level in organisations, families or society in general, leaders feel that they have achieved if the young people who are in the team do well and are successful. This also indicates that leaders don't feel threatened with their success because they were once there and move on to other areas of contribution and achievement. Therefore, generating trust and extending support are important contributions made by effective leaders. However, this is not easy to accomplish.

Trust is anchored in care and concern. Leaders who build trust are also perceived to be caring and supportive and the team is confident that they will always have its well-being in mind. Many a time leaders are seen to be sacrificing their own advantage for the benefit of the team. They also go out of their way to safeguard the rights of the team. The primary roles performed by leaders for trust building is that of gate keeping and boundary management. Gate-keeping wards off negative pressures from the team and helps in maintaining a non-political atmosphere and a fair culture. A sense of fairness is a strong pillar for building trusting relationships. Leaders all over the world and from diverse organisations and communities feel a sense of achievement in establishing such relationships and more so in a world which is complex, with hidden agendas and motives and an orientation to exploit.

Keeping promises also goes a long way in building trust for it creates dependable and reliable relationships. Delegation and sharing responsibility takes place with leaders and teams which are dependable and reliable. Leaders build responsibility in the team by demonstrating it themselves. Therefore, a dependable and reliable leader is trusted, a person who does what he says and who doesn't go back on his word and commitment. Needless to say, responsibilities are only discharged well by those who have the abilities and the competencies to respond effectively. Therefore, leaders know that people must be prepared and coached for assuming responsibility. This happens all the time in nature when the parents amongst animals and birds coach their young to become competent to hunt and take charge of their safety and security as well for food and water. This is done through demonstration, observation, practice even though it is instinctual. Once the young develop skills they are left to fend for themselves and they move on to independence and responsibility. The cycle repeats itself when they become parents and teach and coach their young offsprings. Earning trust is a huge achievement for leaders and leaders even in the corporate sector and the government are being judged by the degree to which they inspire trust amongst people and the members of their organisations. Trust begets trust and is seen to be a major contributing factor for high and exceptional performance of individuals and teams and in fact the organisation.

Respect is commanded and earned by leaders and they consider it their big achievement. With trust, respect, genuineness and warmth are seen as three other pillars on which trusting and long lasting relationships are built. Many leaders consider this as their most significant achievements. They are respected for their knowledge, functional and strategic competence, general managerial capabilities, vision and values, understanding and handling of the environment, their skills to solve problems and manage crisis, their people connect and their human and professional qualities. Respect for the chair and position is different from respect for the human capabilities and qualities of leaders. The more lasting is the latter. It is evident that the long term success and influence of leaders is positively correlated with their earned respect. It is therefore evident, that leaders not only achieve organisational financial targets but also consider building trusting relationships and professional and humanitarian and strong organisational and social cultures as equally important and significant achievements. They make great efforts in nurturing and developing future talent, supporting socially deprived communities and augmenting the happiness index.

The achievement motive creates three or four distinct propensities towards success, risk taking and leadership styles and assumptions. Studies have shown that people select different goals to achieve in life. The drive for achievement determines whether in fact any goal which an individual selects is achieved or not. If the drive to achieve is strong then the goal is normally achieved. However, the achievement motive is a definite building-block for leadership capabilities. Political leaders, social leaders and business leaders all have strong achievement drives even though their area of contribution and goals are different. They are driven by success in their fields and in order that success is obtained they display capabilities for influencing people, decision making, building teams, leading and setting directions for the future, guiding action and execution or doing it themselves and confronting and solving problems. There are two orientations, to approach success and the other is to avoid failure. The achievement motive strengthens the former.